Israel

& the
Palestinian Territories

a Lonely Planet travel atlas

Israel & the Palestinian Territories – travel atlas

1st edition

Published by
Lonely Planet Publications
Head Office: PO Box 617, Hawthorn, Vic 3122, Australia
Branches: 155 Filbert St, Suite 251, Oakland, CA 94607, USA
             10 Barley Mow Passage, Chiswick, London W4 4PH, UK
             71 bis rue du Cardinal Lemoine, 75005 Paris, France

Cartography
Steinhart Katzir Publishers Ltd
Fax: 972-3-699-7562
email: 100264.721@compuserve.com

Printed by
Colorcraft Ltd, Hong Kong

Photographs
Gadi Farfour, Andrew Humphreys, Israeli Ministry of Tourism (IMT)

Front Cover: The Old City walls of Jerusalem (Andrew Humphreys)
Back Cover: 'The Mona Lisa of Galilee', Byzantine-era mosaic (IMT)
Title page: Jaffa harbourside (Andrew Humphreys)
Contents page: The Judean Desert meets the Dead Sea (Andrew Humphreys)

First Published
November 1996

Although the authors and publisher have tried to make the information as accurate as possible, they accept no responsibility for any loss, injury or inconvenience sustained by any person using this book.

National Library of Australia Cataloguing in Publication Data

Humphreys, Andrew, 1965-.
    Israel & the Palestinian Territories travel atlas.

    1st ed.
    Includes index.
    ISBN 0 86442 440 X.

    1. Israel - Maps, Tourist. 2. Palestine - Maps, Tourist.
    3. Israel - Road Maps. 4. Palestine - Road Maps.
    I. Title. (Series : Lonely Planet travel atlas).

912.5694

Contents

Andrew Humphreys

Trained as an architect, Andrew first encountered the Middle East in the form of Egypt in 1988 when a three-week holiday extended to a three-year-long stay. Part of this time he spent documenting Islamic architecture for a Cairo university, later going on to work for *Egypt Today*, the country's biggest English-language periodical.

In 1991, an unexpected turn of events deposited Andrew in newly independent Estonia with a ringside seat from which to observe the aftereffects of the disintegration of the USSR. Initially working for a local English-language paper, Andrew moved on to co-found a new pan-Baltic newspaper, at which point a happy chance meeting with Lonely Planet set him to work as a contributor to the second edition of Lonely Planet's *Scandinavian & Baltic Europe on a Shoestring*. Since then he's covered Siberia for LP's guidebook to *Russia, Ukraine & Belarus*, researched two of the five republics in *Central Asia – travel survival kit* and updated the *Israel & the Palestinian Territories – travel survival kit*.

About this Atlas

This book is another addition to the Lonely Planet travel atlas series. Designed to tie in with the equivalent Lonely Planet guidebook, we hope that the *Israel & the Palestinian Territories travel atlas* helps travellers enjoy their trip even more. As well as detailed, accurate maps, this atlas also contains a multilingual map legend, useful travel information in five languages and a comprehensive index to ensure easy location-finding.

The maps were checked on the road by Andrew Humphreys as part of his preparation for a new edition of Lonely Planet's *Israel & the Palestinian Territories – travel survival kit*.

From the Publishers

Thanks to Danny Schapiro, chief cartographer at Steinhart Katzir Publishers, who supervised production of this atlas. Danna Sharoni was responsible for the cartography. Iris Sardes prepared the index. At Lonely Planet, editorial checking of the maps and index was completed by Lou Byrnes. Sally Jacka was responsible for the cartographic checking. Layout, design and cover design was completed by Louise Keppie-Klep. Paul Smitz edited the getting around text.

Lou Byrnes coordinated the translations. Thanks to translators Yoshiharu Abe, Christa Bouga-Hochstöger, Adrienne Costanzo, Pedro Diaz, Brad Felstead, Sergio Andrés Mariscal, Patricia Matthieu, Isabelle Muller, Karin Riederer and Penelope Richardson.

Request

This atlas is designed to be clear, comprehensive and reliable. We hope you'll find it a worthy addition to your Lonely Planet travel library. Even if you don't, please let us know! We'd appreciate any suggestions you may have to make this product even better. Please complete and send us the feedback page at the back of this atlas to let us know exactly what you think.

Publisher's Note

At the time of production of this book the Gaza Strip and seven West Bank cities (Jericho, Jenin, Nablus, Tulkarem, Qalqilya, Ramallah and Bethlehem) were under the autonomous rule of the Palestinian National Authority. However, the areas under Palestinian self-rule are subject to future political decisions, and the boundaries may change.

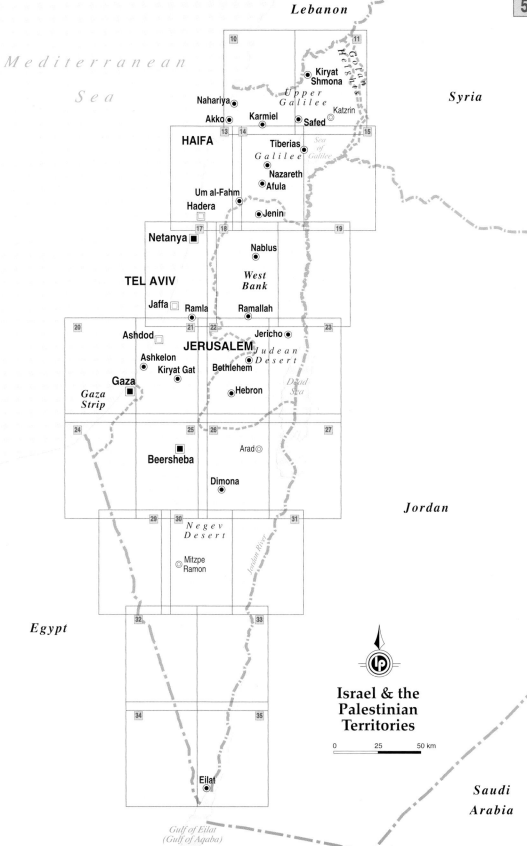

Lebanon

Mediterranean

Sea

Syria

Golan Heights

10

11

Kiryat
Shmona

Upper
Galilee

Nahariya

Katzrin

Akko

Karmiel

Safed

13 14

15

HAIFA

Tiberias

Galilee

Sea
of
Galilee

Nazareth

Afula

Um al-Fahm

Hadera

Jenin

17 18

19

Netanya

Nablus

TEL AVIV

West
Bank

Jaffa

Ramla

Ramallah

20

21 22

23

Ashdod

Jericho

JERUSALEM

Judean
Desert

Ashkelon

Bethlehem

Kiryat Gat

Gaza

Hebron

Dead
Sea

Gaza
Strip

24

25 26

27

Beersheba

Arad

Dimona

Jordan

29 30

31

Negev
Desert

Mitzpe
Ramon

Jordan River

Egypt

32

33

34

35

Israel & the
Palestinian
Territories

0   25   50 km

Eilat

Saudi
Arabia

Gulf of Eilat
(Gulf of Aqaba)

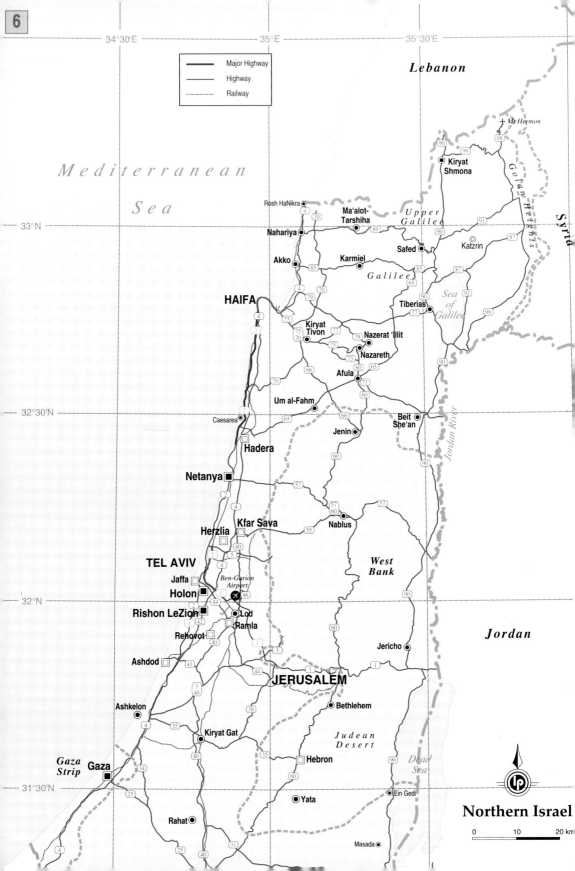

6

Major Highway
Highway
Railway

34°30'E   35°E   35°30'E

Lebanon

Mediterranean

Sea

+ *Mt Hermon*

Kiryat Shmona

Golan Heights

Rosh HaNikra

Ma'alot-Tarshiha

Upper Galilee

33°N

Nahariya

Safed   Katzrin

Akko   Karmiel

Galilee

Syria

HAIFA

Tiberias   *Sea of Galilee*

Kiryat Tivon   Nazerat 'Illit

Nazareth

Afula

Um al-Fahm

32°30'N   Caesarea

Beit She'an

Hadera

Jenin   *Jordan River*

Netanya

Kfar Sava

Herzlia   Nablus

TEL AVIV   *West Bank*

Jaffa   *Ben-Gurion Airport*

Holon

32°N   Rishon LeZion   Lod

Ramla

Rehovot

Jordan

Ashdod   Jericho

JERUSALEM

Ashkelon   Bethlehem

Kiryat Gat   *Judean Desert*

Dead Sea

Hebron

Gaza Strip   Gaza

31°30'N   Yata   Ein Gedi

Northern Israel

Rahat

0   10   20 km

Masada

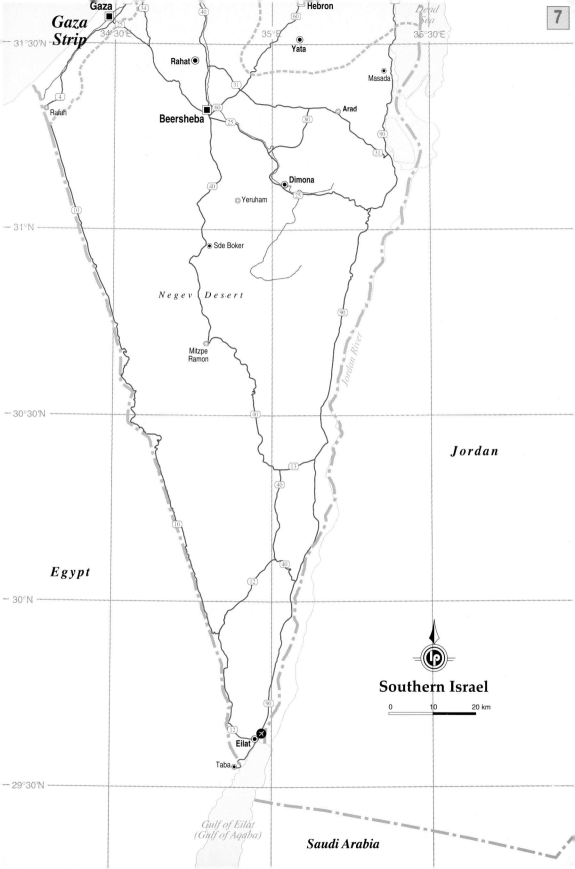

MAP LEGEND

Number of Inhabitants:

TEL AVIV > 250,000

Netanya ■ 100,000 - 250,000

Kfar Sava ☐ 50,000 - 100,000

Naharya ◉ 10,000 - 50,000

Even Yehuda ◎ 2,000 - 10,000

Ga'ton ◉ < 2,000 Kibbutz

Udim ◉ < 2,000 Moshav

Kelil ◉ < 2,000 Village

International Boundary
Limites Internationales
Staatsgrenze
Frontera Internacional
国境

Disputed Boundary
Frontière Contestée
umstrittene Grenze
Frontera Disputada
国境紛争境界線

Major Highway
Route Nationale
Femstraße
Carretera Principal
主要な国道

Highway
Route Principale
Landstraße
Carretera
国道

Regional Road
Route Régionale
Regionale Fernstraße
Carretera Regional
地方道

Secondary Road
Route Secondaire
Nebenstraße
Carretera Secundaria
二級道路

Unsealed Road
Route non bitumée/piste
Unbefestigte Straße
Carretera sin Asfaltar
未舗装の道

Railway
Voie de chemin de fer
Eisenbahn
Ferrocarril
鉄道

40 Distance in Kilometres
Distance en Kilomètres
Entfernung in Kilometern
Distancia en Kilómetros
距離（km)

✈ International Airport
Aéroport International
Internationaler Flughafen
Aeropuerto Internacional
国際空港

✈ Domestic Airport
Aéroport National
Inlandflughafen
Aeropuerto Interior
国内線空港

Seaport
Port de Mer
Seehafen
Puerto Marítimo
港

☪	Mosque Mosquée Moschee Mezquita モスク	*Mt Meiron* *1208* ÷	Mountain Montagne Berg Montaña 山	|||	Waterfall Cascades Wasserfall Catarata 滝
†	Church Église Kirche Iglesia 教会	⛱	National Park Parc National Nationalpark Parque Nacional 国立公園		Desert Désert Wüste Desierto 砂漠
✡	Synagogue Synagogue Synagoge Sinagoga ユダヤ教会	⛺	Camping Ground Terrain de Camping Zeltplatz Camping キャンプ場		Reef Falaise Riff Arrecife 岩礁
⛰	Monument Monument Denkmal Monumento 記念碑	⛷	Ski Field Domaine Skiable Skipiste Campo para esquiar スキー場		Swamp Marais Sumpf Pantano 沼地
🏛	Palace Palais Palast Palacio 宮殿	◆✦	Border Crossing Frontières Grenzübergang Cruce de Frontera 国境越え地点		Salt Lake Lac Salé Salzsee Lago de Sal 塩湖
∴	Ruins Ruines Ruinen Ruinas 遺跡	～	River Fleuve/Rivière Fluß Río 川		4000 m 3500 m 3000 m 2500 m
※	Viewpoint Point de Vue Aussicht Mirador 展望地点	～	Wadi Wadi Wadi Uadi ワジ		2100 m 1800 m 1500 m 1200 m 900 m
○	Beach Plage Strand Playa 海岸	⬭	Lake Lac See Lago 湖		600 m 300 m 150 m 0
◣	Cave Grotte Höhle Cueva 洞窟	⊶	Spring Source Quelle Manantial 泉		-100 m -200 m -300 m -400 m

0   2   4   6   8   10 km

1 : 250 000

Lambert Conformal
Conic projection

Largely unspoilt by tourism, there is no city more timeless than Akko

Column Headers
E   F   G   H

35°E

13

▲10▲

Row 1

Kfar Masaryk

Zevulun Valley

Ein Nimfit Reserve

Haifa Bay

Kiryat Yam

Kiryat Bialik

Ein Afek Reserve

Afek

Kiryat Mozkin

Kfar Bialik

Zaid

HAIFA
חיפה

Tel Shikmona

Kiryat Ata

Usha

Ramat Yohanan

Row 2

Shikmona Interchange

Nahal 'Ovadya

Nesher

Mt Carmel

Nahal Qishon

Kfar HaMaccabi

Hurvat Sasay

Kfar Galim

Tirat Karmel

Nahal Nesher Reserve

Tel Regev

Ibtin

HaHotrim

Ornit Cave

HaKarmel Park

Yagur

Rekhasim

Sha'ar Ha'Amakim Reserve

Hof 'Atlit Reserve

Beit Oren

Kfar Hasidim

Sha'ar Ha'Amakim

Row 3

Sfonim Cave

Megadim

Mt Oren 301

Mt Alon 515

Mt Alon Reserve

Isfiya

Kiryat Tivon

Alonim

'Atlit Interchange

Me'arat Oren

Daliyat al-Karmel

Mt Shokef 497

Hurvat Serak

Beit Zaid

Beit She'arim Reserve

'Atlit

Ein Hod

Nir 'Ezyon

Hurvat Dabla

Hurvat Ali ad-Din

Sde Ya'acov

Neve Yam

Ein Karmel

Nahal Me'arot Reserve

Mt Mehalel 458

Somek Cave

Hurvat Muhraqa

Yokne'am Illit

Nahal Qishon

Geva' Karmel

HaKarmel Cave

Hurvat Hermesh

Zarufa

Kerem Maharal Reserve

Kerem Maharal

Hurvat Dereg

Rakefet Cave

HaZorea

Row 4

The Blue Cave

HaBonim

Ein Ayala

Maharal Valley

Elyakim

Ein HaEmek

Ramat HaShofet

Tel Shosh

Nahsholim

Ofer

Hurvat Talimon

Nahal Daliya Reserve

Ein HaSholet

Mishmar HaEmek

Dor

Meir Shefeya

Bat Shlomo

Mt Horshan Reserve

Ramot Menashe

Daliya

Zichron Ya'acov Interchange

Fureidis

Ramat HaNadiv National Park

Zichron Ya'acov

Mt Horshan 178

Ma'yan Zevi

Row 5

Kabara Cave

Ma'agan Michael

Ya'ar Alona Reserve

Amikam

Giv'at Nili

Even Yitzhak

Nahal Taninim Reserve

'Ein Ibrahim

Mu'awiya

Jisr es-Zarqa

Beit Hananya

Nahal HaNadiv

Binyamina

Aviel

Nahal Taninim

Giv'at 'Ada

Regavim

Um al-Fahm

Or Akiva

Alonei Yitzhak

Kafr Qari'a

'Ara

Caesarea Reserve

Caesarea

Kfar Glickson

Me'... Amm...

Ar'ara

'Ein es Sahia

Sdot Yam

Alon Binyamina Reserve

Mishmarot

Nahal Barkan

Nadiv Valley

Kazir

Row 6

Kfar Pines

Ein Iron

Barkal

Iron Hills

Hurvat Tawila

Barta'a

Rehan

Caesarea Interchange

Pardes Hana Karkur

Gan Shomeron

Ein Shemer

Um al-Qutuf

Zibda

Gan Shemuel

Ma'anit

Olga Interchange

Talmei El'azar

Sha'ar Menashe

Meisir

Mezzer

Qaffin

Hermesh

Hadera
חדרה

Tel Zror

Ma'or

Baq'a al-Gharbiya

Baqa Sharqiya

Nahal Hadera

▼17▼

Mikhmoret

Elyakhin

Sde Yizhak

Nazlat 'Isa

▼18▼

Tel Girit

Herev Le'et

Giv'at Hayim (Ihud)

Lehavot Haviva

Jat

Nazlat

Hibat Zion

Ge'ule Teman

Kfar HaRo'e

Giv'at Hayim (Me'uhad)

Ahituv

Tel Jatt

Seida

Hofit

Kfar Vitkin

En HaHoresh

Magal

Zeita

Bet Yanai

Beit Herut

Hogla

Ne'urim

Elyashiv

Hefer Valley

HaMa'pil

Nahal Alexander

32°30'N

Mediterranean Sea

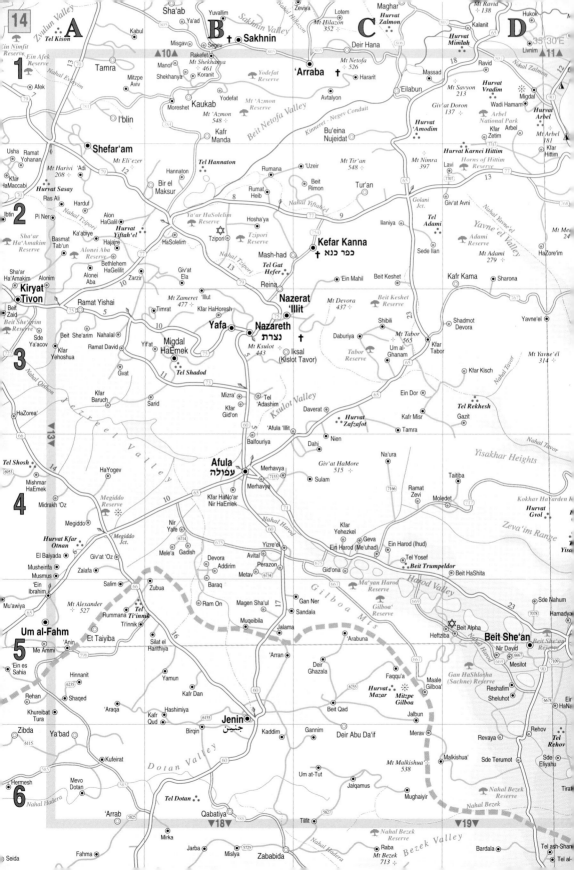

The Russian Orthodox Church of the Holy Trinity in Jerusalem

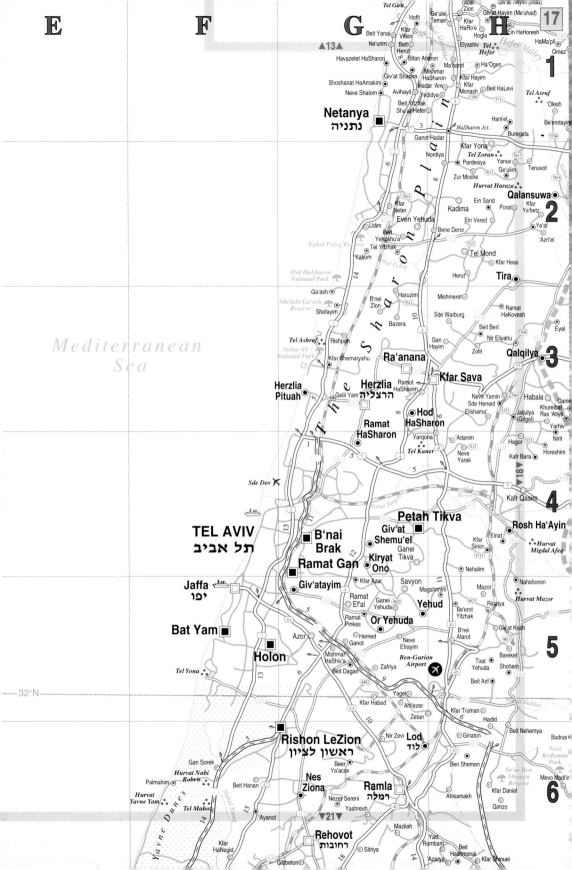

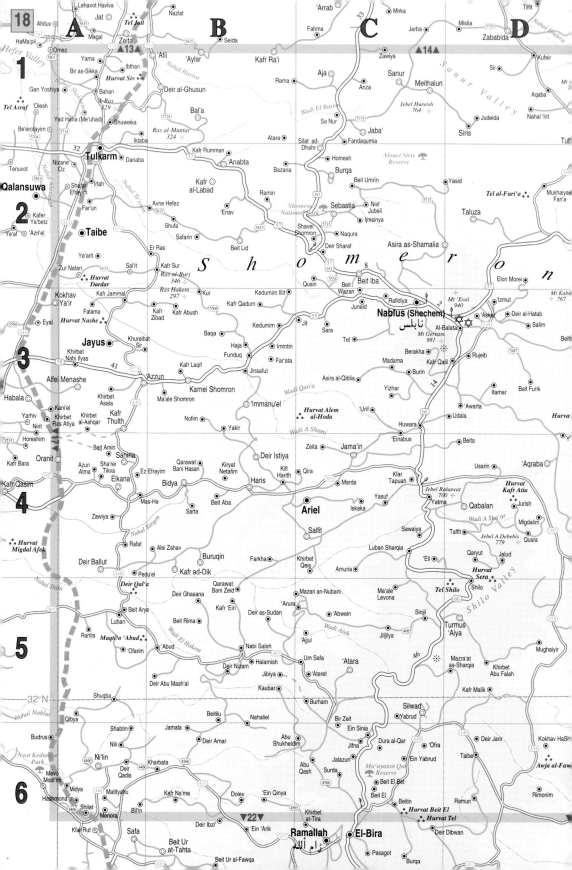

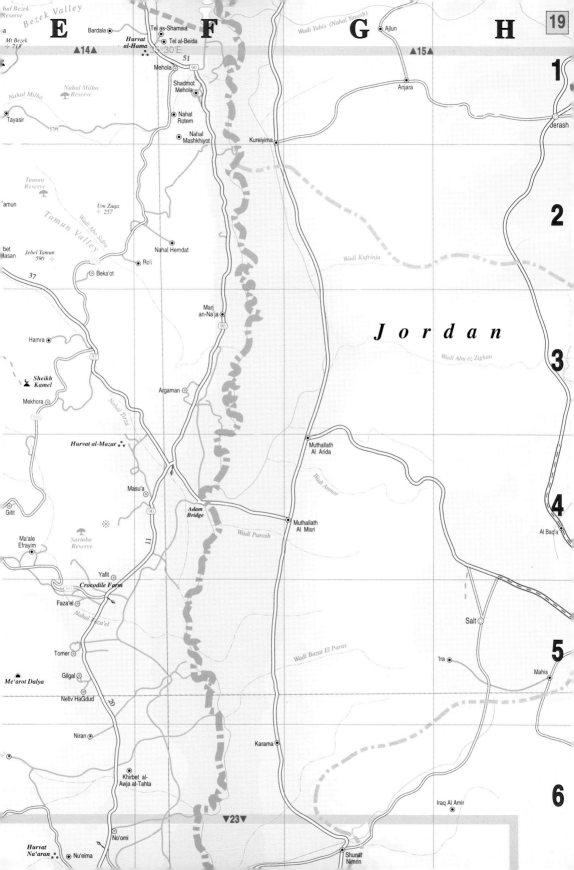

	A	B	C	D

A **B** **C** **D**

34°30'E

▲16▲

1

2

Mediterranean
Sea

3

4

Elei Sinai

Dugit

Atatra

Nazla

5

Jabalia

G a z a
S t r i p

Gaza ■
غزه

Qoba

Nezarim

31°30'N

Nahal 'Oz

Nuseirat

Bureij

Bitronot Be'eri
Reserve

6

▼24▼

Deir al-Balah

Be'eri

23

Mughazi

Wadi Abu Qatarun

Nahal Salqa

Kfar Darom

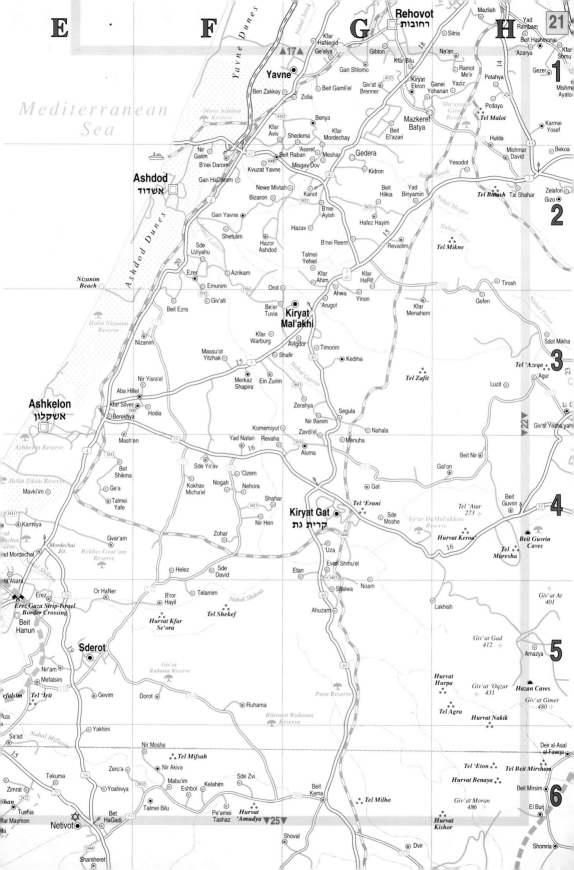

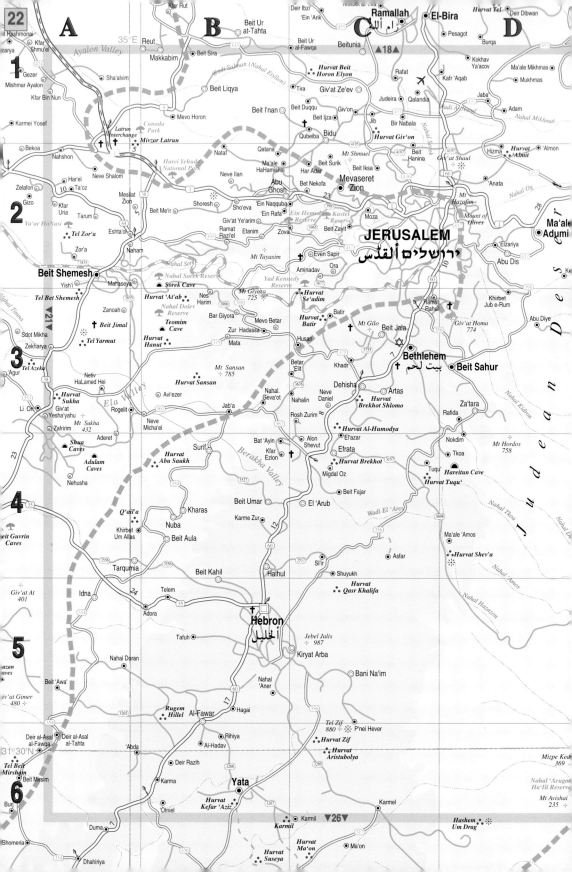

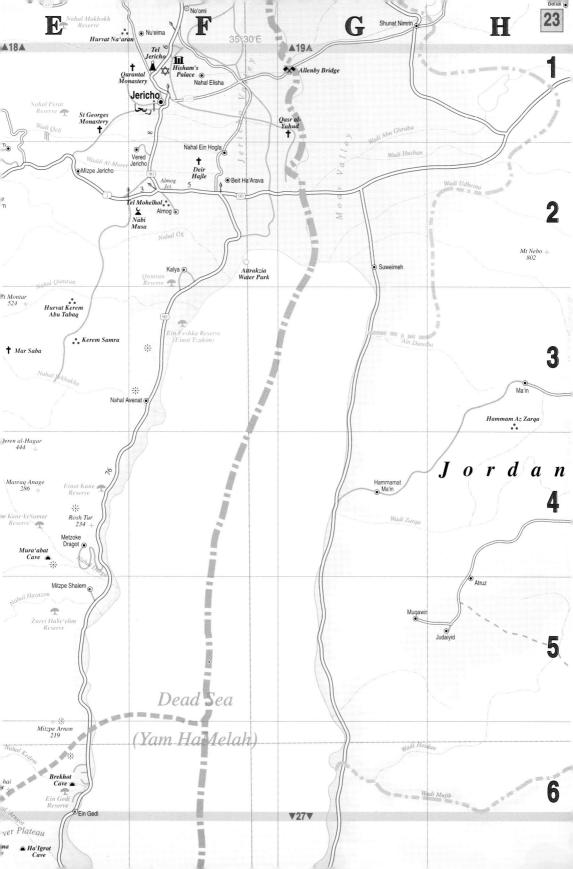

Baliai

Nahal Makhokh Reserve

No'omi

Nu'eima

Hurvat Na'aran

Shunat Nimrin

▲18▲   35°30'E   ▲19▲

Tel Jericho

Allenby Bridge

Qarantal Monastery

Hisham's Palace

Nahal Elisha

1

Jericho أريحا

St Georges Monastery

Qasr al-Yahud

Nahal Perat Reserve

Wadi Qelt

Wadi Abu Ghraba

Nahal Ein Hogla

Wadi Husban

Vered Jericho

Waddi Al-Morer

Mizpe Jericho

Deir Hajle

Wadi Udheimi

2

Almog Jct.

Beit Ha'Arava

90

3   5

Tel Mohelhol

Nabi Musa

Almog

Nahal Og

Moav Valley

Mt Nebo 802

Kalya

Attrakzia Water Park

Suweimeh

Nahal Qumran

Qumran Reserve

t Montar 524

Hurvat Kerem Abu Tabaq

90

Kerem Samra

Ein Feshka Reserve (Einot Tzukim)

'Ain Dureiba

3

Mar Saba

Nahal Sekhakha

Ma'in

Hammam Az Zarqa

Nahal Avenat

Deren al-Hagar 444

J o r d a n

Masraq Anage 286

Einot Kane Reserve

76

Hammamat Ma'in

4

t Kane-VeSamar Reserve

Rosh Tur 234

Wadi Zarqa

Metzoke Dragot

Mura'abat Cave

Nahal Darga

Atruz

Mitzpe Shalem

Nahal Hazazon

Muqawir

Zurei HaYe'elim Reserve

Judaiyid

5

Dead Sea

(Yam HaMelah)

Mitzpe Arnon 219

Wadi Heidan

Nahal Kedem

Brekhot Cave

Ein Gedi Reserve

Wadi Mujib

6

Ein Gedi

r Plateau

Ha'Igrot Cave

▼27▼

A B C D

1

2

3

4

5

6

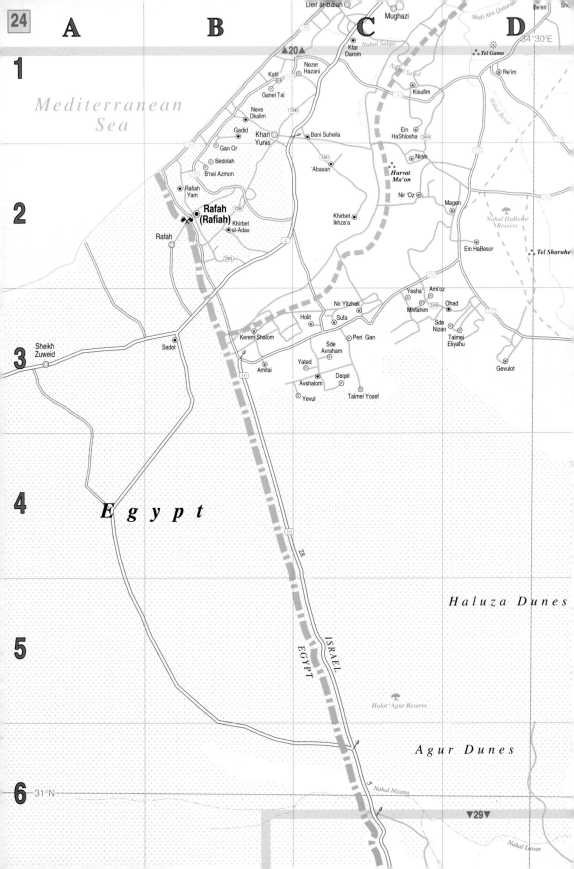

Mediterranean Sea

Deir al-Balah
Mughazi
Nahal Salqa
Kfar Darom
▲20▲
Klar Darom
Nezer Hazani
Katif
Ganei Tal
Neve Dkalim
Gadid
Khan Yunis
Gan Or
Bedolah
B'nei Azmon
Rafiah Yam
Rafah (Rafiah)
Khirbet al-Adas
Rafah
Bani Suheila
'Abasan
Khirbet Ikhza'a
Tel Gama
Re'im
Kisufim
Ein HaShlosha
Nirim
Hurvat Ma'on
Nir 'Oz
Magen
Nahal HaBesor Reserve
Ein HaBesor
Tel Sharuhe
Yesha'
Ami'oz
Mivtahim
Ohad
Sde Nizan
Talmei Eliyahu
Nir Yitzhak
Holit
Sufa
Peri Gan
Kerem Shalom
Sde Avraham
Gevulot
Sheikh Zuweid
Sadot
Amitai
Yated
Deqel
Avshalom
Talmei Yosef
Yevul

34°30'E

Nahal Sa'ed

Nahal Besor

Wadi Abu Qatarun

Be'eri

E g y p t

ISRAEL
EGYPT

Haluza Dunes

Holot 'Agur Reserve

Agur Dunes

31°N

Nahal Nizana

▼29▼

Nahal Lavan

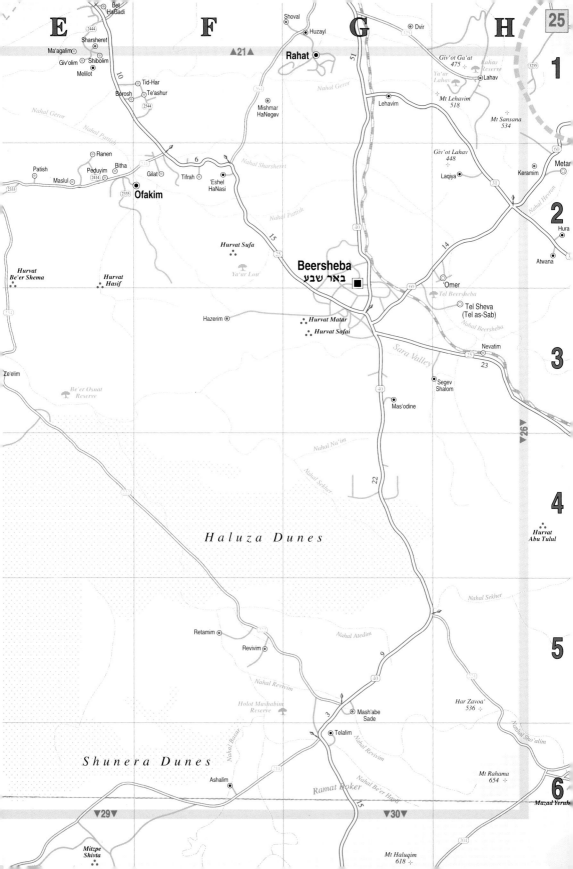

E **F** **G** **H**

1
2
3
4
5
6

Bet HaGadi
Shoval
Dvir
Sharsheret
Huzayl
Ma'agalim
Rahat
Giv'ot Ga'at 475
Lahav Reserve
Giv'olim
Shibolim
Ya'ar Lahav
Lahav
Melilot
Lehavim
Mt Lehavim 518
Tid-Har
Te'ashur
Berosh
Mt Sansana 534
▲21▲

Mishmar HaNegev
Giv'ot Lahav 448
Metar
Ranen
Keramim
Patish
Bitha
Gilat
Laqiya
Peduyim
Tifrah
Maslul
'Eshel HaNasi
Hura
Ofakim

Atwana
Hurvat Be'er Shema
Hurvat Sufa
Hurvat Hasif
Beersheba
באר שבע
'Omer
Tel Beersheba
Ya'ar Lou
Tel Sheva (Tel as-Sab)
Hazerim
Hurvat Matar
Hurvat Safai
Nahal Beersheba

Sara Valley
Nevatim
Ze'elim
23
Be'er Osnat Reserve
Segev Shalom
Mas'odine

Nahal Na'im
Nahal Sekher

H a l u z a   D u n e s
Hurvat Abu Tulul

Nahal Sekher

Retamim
Revivim
Nahal Atedim
Har Zavoa' 536
Nahal Revivim
Holot Mashabim Reserve
Mash'abe Sade
S h u n e r a   D u n e s
Telalim
Nahal Besor
Nahal Revivim
Mt Rahama 654
Ashalim
Ramat Boker
Mt Haluqim 618
Mitzpe Shivta
Mazad Yeruh

▼29▼
▼30▼
◄26►

Nahal Geror
Nahal Patish
Nahal Geror
Nahal Sharsheret
Nahal Patish
Nahal Hevron

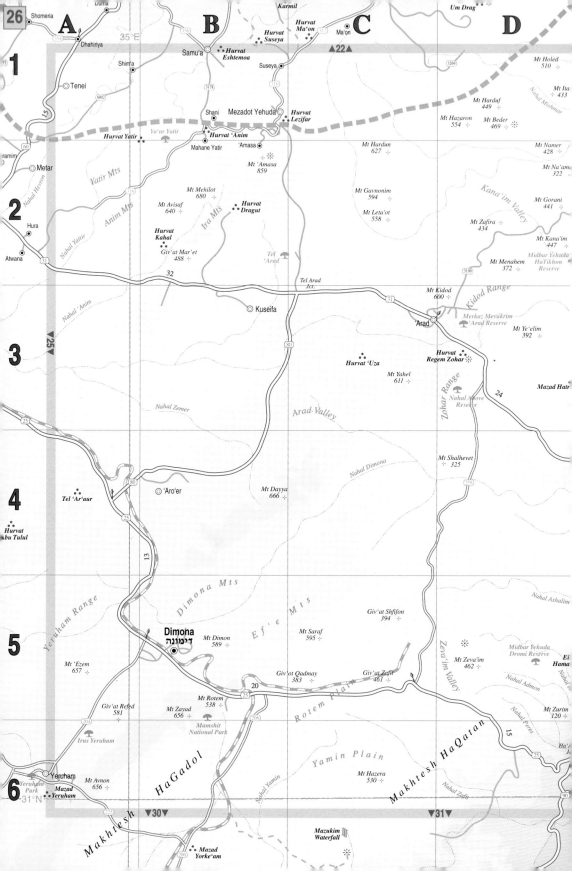

26

A   B   C   D

1

Shomeria
Duma
Karmil
Um Drag
Dhahiriya
35°E
Samu'a
Hurvat Suseya
Hurvat Ma'on
Ma'on
▲22▲
Shim'a
Hurvat Eshtemoa
Suseya
Mt Holed 510
Tenei
Mt Ita 433
Mt Harduf 449
Nahal Mishmar
Mezadot Yehuda
Hurvat Lezifar
Shani
Mt Hazaron 554
Mt Beder 469 ☼

2

Hurvat Yatir
Ya'ar Yatir
Hurvat 'Anim
Hurvat Yitir
Mahane Yatir
'Amasa
Mt Namer 428
ramim
Metar
Yatir Mts
Nahal Hevron
Mt 'Amasa 859
Mt Hardun 627 ÷
Mt Na'am 322
Mt Mehilot 680
Anim Mts
Ira Mts
Mt Gavnonim 594
Kana'im Valley
Mt Gorani 441
Mt Avisaf 640
Hurvat Dragut
Mt Leta'ot 558
Mt Zafira 434
Hura
Nahal Yattir
Hurvat Kahal
Giv'at Mar'et 488
Tel 'Arad
Mt Kana'im 447
Atwana
32
Tel Arad Jct.
Mt Menahem 372
Midbar Yehuda HaTikhon Reserve
(3199)

3

▼25▼
Nahal 'Anim
Kuseifa
31
Mt Kidod 600
Kidod Range
Merkaz Mevakrim 'Arad Reserve
Arad
Mt Ye'elim 392 ÷
Nahal Zemer
80
Hurvat 'Uza
Hurvat Regem Zohar ☼
Zohar Range
24
Mazad Hatr
Mt Yahel 611 ÷
Arad-Valley
Nahal Above Reserve

4

25
Nahal Dimona
Mt Shalhevet 325 ÷
80
'Aro'er
Mt Dayya 666 ÷
Tel 'Ar'aur
Hurvat bu Tulul
13
Yeruham Range

5

Dimona Mts
E f ' e   M t s
Giv'at Shfifon 394 ÷
Nahal Ashalim
Dimona
דימונה
Mt Dimon 589
Mt Saraf 595
☼
Midbar Yehuda Dromi Reserve
Ei Hama
Mt 'Ezem 657
Giv'ot Qadmay 383
Giv'at Zafit 461
Mt Zeva'im 462
Zeva'im Valley
Nahal Admon
Giv'at Refed 581
Mt Rotem 538
20
25
Rotem Plain
Nahal Peres
Mt Zurim 120
Mt Zayad 656
Mamshit National Park
15
Irus Yeruham
204

6

Yeruham Park
Yeruham
31°N
Mt Avnon 656
Mazad Yeruham
HaGadol
Yamin Plain
Mt Hazera 530 ÷
Makhtesh HaQatan
Nahal Yamin
Nahal Zafir
90
Makhtesh
▼30▼
▼31▼
Mazad Yorke'am
Mazukim Waterfall

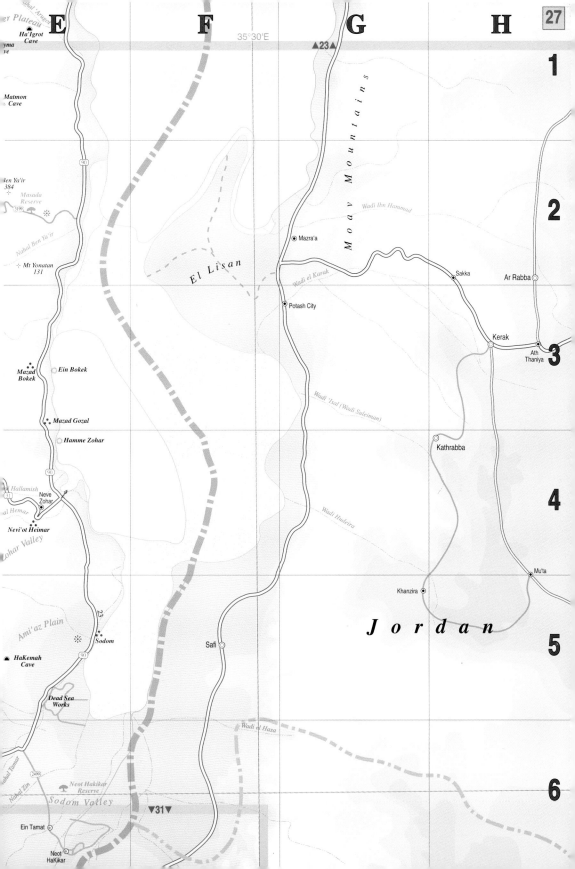

Completed in 691, the Dome of the Rock is a unique confection of pink-veined marble, peacock mosaics and gold leaf

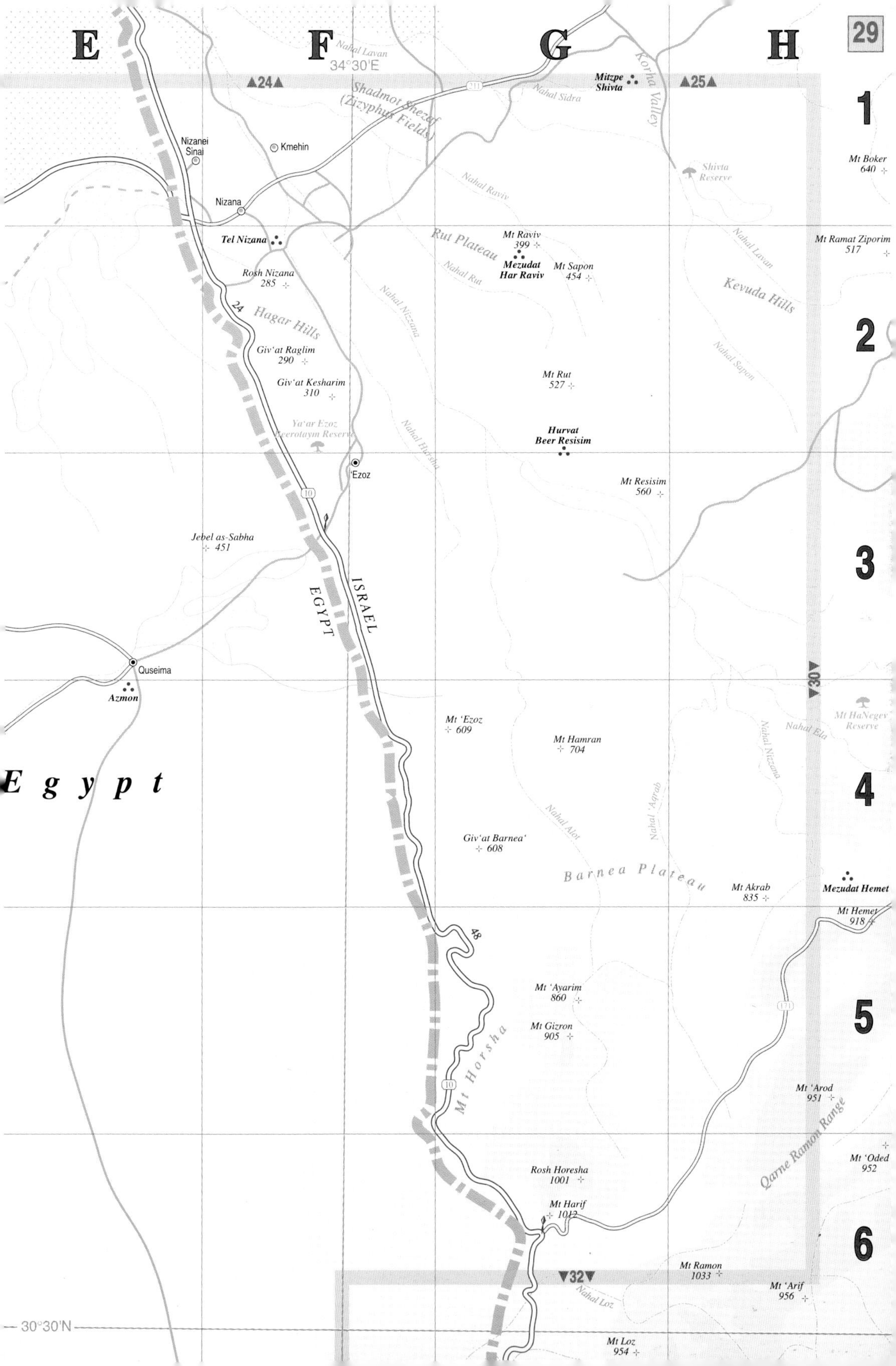

E F 34°30'E G H

Nahal Lavan

E **F** **G** **H**

1

▲24▲ Shadmot Shezaf *Nahal Sidra* **Mitzpe Shivta** ∴ ▲25▲
(*Ziziphus Fields*)

Nizanei Sinai

Kmehin Shivta Reserve Mt Boker 640

Nizana *Nahal Raviv* *Korha Valley*

Tel Nizana ∴ *Rut Plateau* Mt Raviv 399 ∴ Kevuda Hills Mt Ramat Ziporim 517

Rosh Nizana 285 **Mezudat Har Raviv** Mt Sapon 454 ∴ *Nahal Lavan*

2

24 Hagar Hills *Nahal Nizzana* *Nahal Rut*

Giv'at Raglim 290 Mt Rut 527 ∴ *Nahal Sapon*

Giv'at Kesharim 310 *Nahal Hatira* **Hurvat Beer Resisim** ∴∴

Ya'ar Ezoz Peerotaym Reserve Ezoz Mt Resisim 560 ∴

3

Jebel as-Sabha 451 ∴

EGYPT **ISRAEL**

Quseima Mt 'Ezoz 609 ∴ Mt HaNegev Reserve

Azmon Mt Hamran 704 ∴ *Nahal Nizzana* ▲30▲

4

E g y p t Giv'at Barnea' 608 ∴ *Nahal Alot* *Nahal Arava* *Nahal Ela*

Barnea Plateau Mt Akrab 835 **Mezudat Hemet** ∴∴

Mt Hemet 918 ∴

48 Mt 'Ayarim 860 Mt Horsha Mt Gizron 905

5

Mt 'Arod 951

10 Qarne Ramon Range Mt 'Oded 952

Rosh Horesha 1001 Mt Harif 1012

6

▼32▼ Mt Ramon 1033 Mt 'Arif 956

Nahal Loz

30°30'N Mt Loz 954

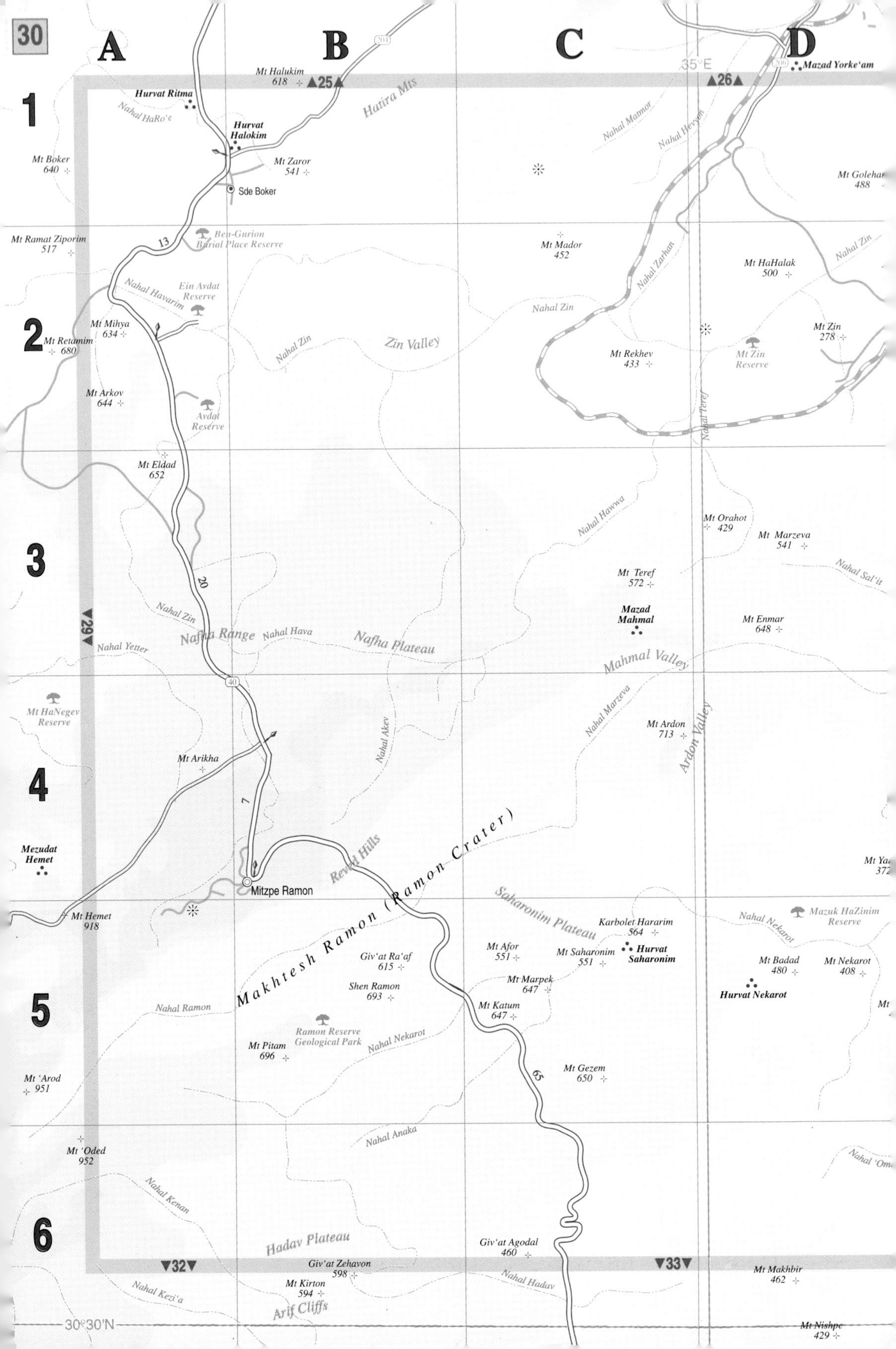

A   **B**   **C**   **D**

1

Mt Halukim
618   ▲25▲

35° E   ▲26▲   Mazad Yorke'am

Hurvat Ritma

Nahal HaRo'e

Hatira Mts

Nahal Mamor

Nahal Hevyon

Hurvat
Halokim

Mt Zaror
541

Mt Boker
640

Sde Boker

Mt Golehar
488

Nahal Zin

2

Mt Ramat Ziporim
517

Ben-Gurion
Burial Place Reserve

Mt Mador
452

Nahal Zafran

Mt HaHalak
500

Nahal Zin

Nahal Havarim

Ein Avdat
Reserve

Mt Mihya
634

Nahal Zin

Zin Valley

Nahal Zin

Mt Rekhev
433

Mt Zin
Reserve

Mt Zin
278

Mt Retamim
680

Mt Arkov
644

Avdat
Reserve

Nahal Paran

3

Mt Eldad
652

Nahal Hawwa

Mt Orahot
429

Mt Marzeva
541

Nahal Sal'it

20

Mt Teref
572

Mt Enmar
648

Nahal Zin

Nafha Range

Nahal Hava

Nafha Plateau

Mazad
Mahmal

▼29▼

Nahal Yetter

Mahmal Valley

4

40

Mt HaNegev
Reserve

Nahal Marzeva

Mt Ardon
713

Ardon Valley

Mt Arikha

7

Nahal Akev

Mezudat
Hemet

Revivim Hills

Mt Ya
372

Mitzpe Ramon

Saharonim Plateau

Karbolet Hararim
564

Nahal Nekarot

Mazuk HaZinim
Reserve

5

Mt Hemet
918

Mt Afor
551

Mt Saharonim
551

Hurvat
Saharonim

Mt Badad
480

Mt Nekarot
408

Makhtesh Ramon (Ramon Crater)

Giv'at Ra'af
615

Mt Marpek
647

Hurvat Nekarot

Mt

Nahal Ramon

Shen Ramon
693

Mt Katum
647

Ramon Reserve
Geological Park

Mt Pitam
696

Nahal Nekarot

65

Mt Gezem
650

Mt 'Arod
951

Nahal Anaka

6

Mt 'Oded
952

Nahal Kenan

Hadav Plateau

▼32▼

Giv'at Zehavon
598

Giv'at Agodal
460

▼33▼

Mt Makhbir
462

Nahal 'Om

Nahal Kezi'a

Mt Kirton
594

Arif Cliffs

Nahal Hadav

30°30'N

Mt Nishpe
429

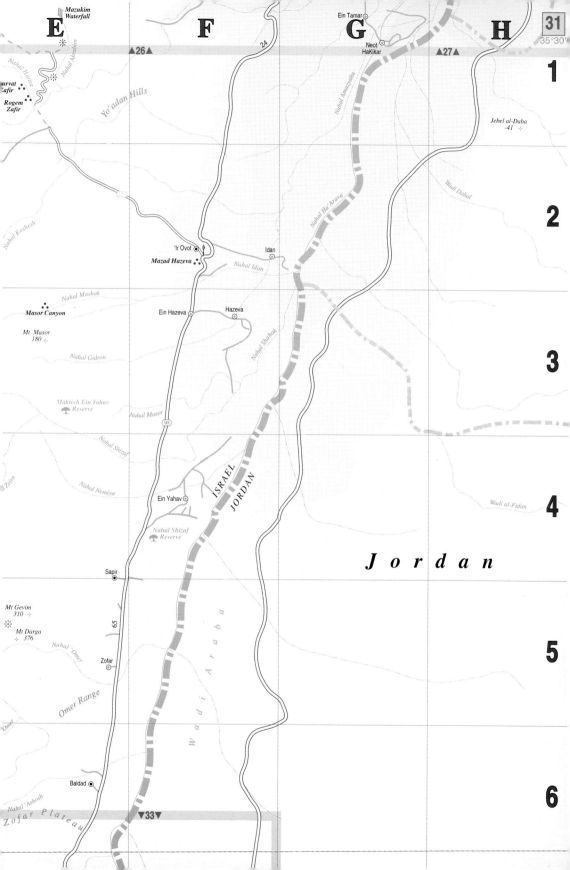

Mazukim
Waterfall

▲26▲   24   Ein Tamar   ▲27▲

1

Neot
HaKikar

Nahal Haziza

Nahal Akrabim

urvat
Zafir

*Rogem
Zafir*

Yo'adan Hills

Jebel al-Daba
-41

Nahal Amazyahu

Wadi Dahal

2

Nahal Koshesh

'Ir Ovot

Idan

Mazad Hazeva

Nahal Idan

Nahal Ho'Arava

Nahal Mashak

Masor Canyon

Ein Hazeva

Hazeva

Mt Masor
180

Nahal Shahak

3

Nahal Gidron

Maktesh Ein Yahav
Reserve

Nahal Masor

901

Nahal Shizaf

l Zina

Nahal Nemiya

Ein Yahav

ISRAEL

JORDAN

Wadi al-Fidan

4

Nahal Shizaf
Reserve

J o r d a n

Sapir

Wadi Araba

Mt Gevim
310

65

Mt Darga
376

Nahal 'Omer

5

Zofar

Omer Range

'Omer

Baldad

Nahal 'Ashosh

6

Zofar Plateau

▼33▼

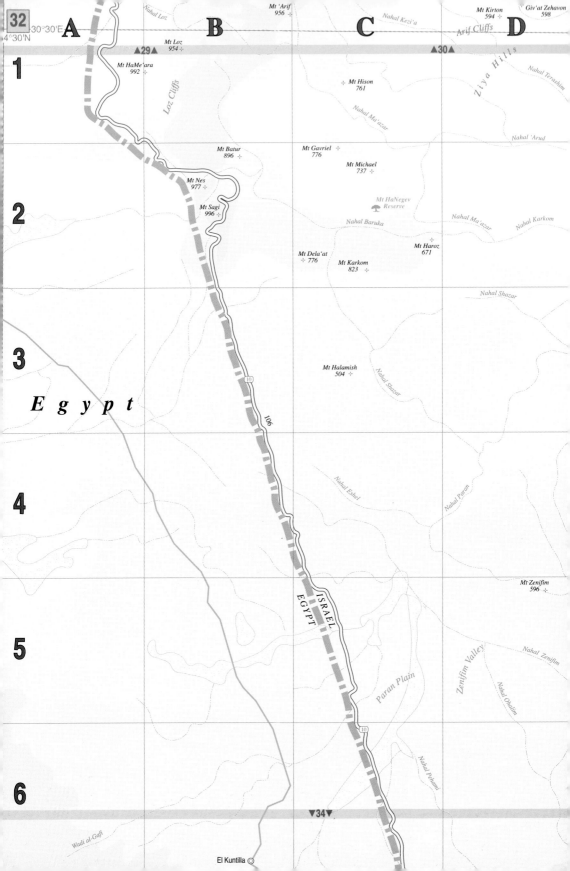

30°30'E
4°30'N

A   **B**   **C**   **D**

Nahal Loz
Mt 'Arif
956
Nahal Kezi'a
Arif Cliffs
Mt Kirton
594
Giv'at Zehavon
598

▲29▲ Mt Loz
954

1
Mt HaMe'ara
992

Loz Cliffs

Mt Hison
761

▲30▲

Ziya Hills

Nahal Terashim

Nahal Ma'azar

Nahal 'Arud

Mt Batur
896

Mt Gavriel
776

Mt Michael
737

Mt Nes
977

Mt HaNegev
Reserve

2
Mt Sagi
996

Nahal Baruka

Nahal Ma'azar

Nahal Karkom

Mt Dela'at
776

Mt Haroz
671

Mt Karkom
823

Nahal Shazar

3

Mt Halamish
504

Nahal Shazar

E g y p t

10

106

Nahal Eshel

Nahal Paran

4

Mt Zenifim
596

ISRAEL
EGYPT

5

Zenifim Valley

Nahal Zenifim

Paran Plain

Nahal Ohalim

6

10

▼34▼

Nahal Pehami

Wadi al-Gafi

El Kuntilla ◎

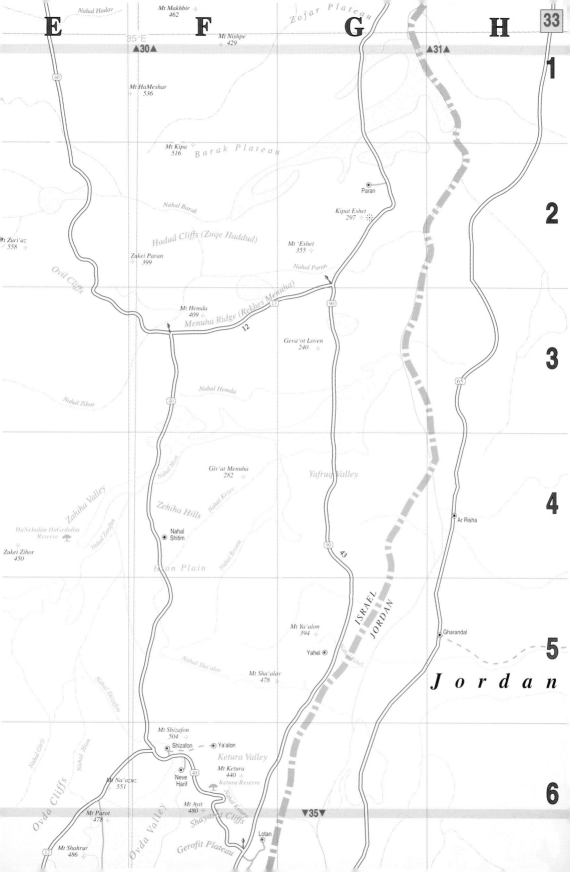

E   F   G   H

Nahal Hadav

Mt Makhbir
462

Zofar Plateau

1

85°E   ▲30▲   Mt Nishpe
429   ▲31▲

40

Mt HaMeshar
536

Mt Kipa
516   *Barak Plateau*

2

Nahal Barak   Paran ☉

Kipat Eshet
297 ☼

t Zuri'az
558   *Hadud Cliffs (Zuqe Haddud)*   Mt 'Eshet
355

Zukei Paran
399   *Nahal Paran*

Ovil Cliffs

Mt Hemda
409   *Menuha Ridge (Rekhes Menuha)*   11   90   3

12   Geva'ot Loven
240

Nahal Zihor   *Nahal Hemda*   40   65

4

Giv'at Menuha
282   *Yafruq Valley*

Zahha Valley   *Zehiha Hills*   Ar Risha

HaNekhalim HaGedolim
Reserve 🌳   Nahal
Shitim   90   43

Zukei Zihor
450

Hion Plain

I
S
R
A
E
L   J
O
R
D
A
N   Gharandal   5

Mt Ya'alon
394

Yahel ☉   ***J o r d a n***

Nahal Sha'alav   Mt Sha'alav
478

Mt Shizafon
504   Shizafon ☉   Ya'alon

Ketura Valley

Mt Na'azuz
551   Neve
Harif   40   Mt Ketura
440

6

Ovda Cliffs   *Ovda Valley*   Mt Ayit
480   Ketura Reserve   ▼35▼

Mt Parot
478   *Shayarot Cliffs*

Mt Shahrur
486   *Gerofit Plateau*   Lotan ☉

12

A B C D

1

30°N

El Kuntilla ◎

▲32▲

Wadi al-Hasa

Mt Hagen
641 ⊹

Mitzpe Sayarim
666 ⊹※⊹

2

Jebel Suweiqa
742 ⊹

Nahal Bik'atayim

Sayarim Valley

ISRAEL

EGYPT

12

3

Mt Bosmat
847 ⊹

Nahal Shani

Mt Seguv
867 ⊹

4

E g y p t

Mt Shani
894 ⊹

Se'ifim P

45

5

Mt Hiz
8

Nahal

✈

Ras an-Naqb ◉

Mt Yoash
734 ⊹

1

6

Mt Reh
38

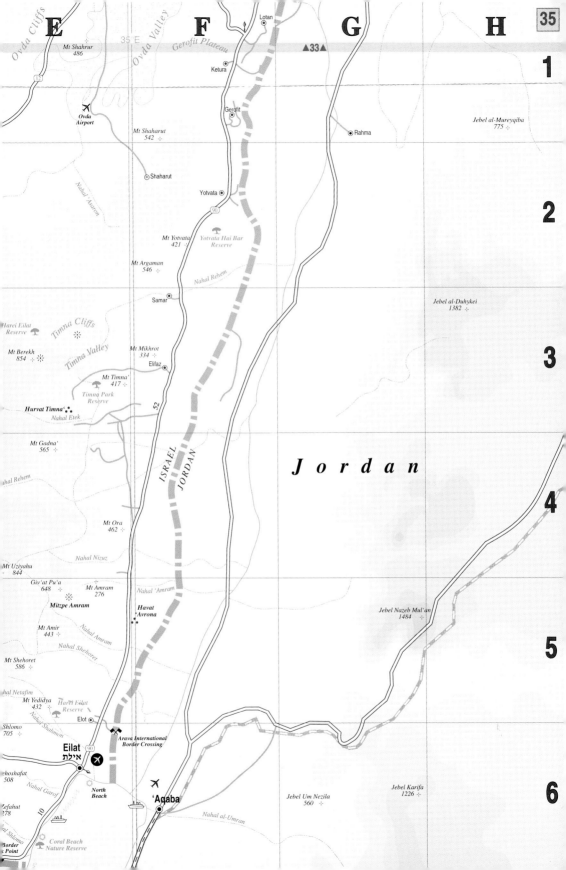

Ovda Cliffs

35 E

Gerofit Plateau

Lotan

▲33▲

Mt Shahrur
486

Ovda Valley

Ketura

✈ **Ovda
Airport**

Gerofit

Rahma

*Jebel al-Mureyqiba
775* ÷

Mt Shaharut
542 ÷

Nahal Asaron

Shaharut

Yotvata

90

Mt Yotvata
421 ÷

*Yotvata Hai Bar
Reserve*

Mt Argaman
546 ÷

Nahal Rehem

*Jebel al-Duhykei
1382* ÷

*Harei Eilat
Reserve*

Timna Cliffs

Samar

÷

Mt Berekh
854 ÷

Timna Valley

Mt Mikhrot
334 ÷

Elifaz

*Jebel al-Duhykei
1382* ÷

Mt Timna'
417 ÷

*Timna Park
Reserve*

52

Hurvat Timna' ∴

Nahal Etek

Mt Gadna'
565 ÷

I S R A E L

J O R D A N

J o r d a n

Nahal Rehem

Mt Ora
462 ÷

Nahal Nizuz

Mt Uziyahu
844

Giv'at Pu'a
648 ÷

Mt Amram
276

Nahal 'Amram

Mitzpe Amram

**Havat
Avrona**

*Jebel Nazeb Mul'an
1484* ÷

Mt Amir
443 ÷

Nahal Amram

Nahal Shehoret

Mt Shehoret
586 ÷

hal Netafim

Mt Yedidya
432 ÷

*Harei Eilat
Reserve*

Elot

Nahal Shahmon

Shlomo
705 ÷

⚒ **Arava International
Border Crossing**

Eilat
אילת

✈

90

*hoshafat
508*

✈

'Aqaba

Nahal Garof

**North
Beach**

1 km

*Jebel Um Nezila
560* ÷

*Jebel Karifa
1226* ÷

*Zefahut
278*

10

Nahal al-Shlomo

Nahal al-Umran

**Border
s Point**

**Coral Beach
Nature Reserve**

Getting Around Israel & the Palestinian Territories

Bus

The relatively small size of Israel combined with an excellent road system make travel by bus *the* way to get around.

Israel's bus network is dominated by Egged, the second-largest bus company in the world after Greyhound. It operates about 4000 buses on over 3000 scheduled routes, as well as numerous special trips. Buses are frequent, fast and well looked after, although booking in advance is recommended for Dead Sea and Negev routes on which Egged doubles as a military transporter, ferrying soldiers to and from their bases.

Most services operate from about 5.30 am to about 10.30 pm daily but beware of Shabbat – on Friday and the eve of Jewish holidays all buses, urban and inter-city, run only until 3 or 4 pm and on Saturday services don't resume until sunset.

Israel's bus system is not the absolute bargain it used to be (what is?) but it's still cheap. The most lengthy journey that the average visitor makes is the run between Eilat and Jerusalem (four hours) or Tel Aviv (five hours) which costs 42 or 46 NIS respectively, or roughly around four US cents per km. On inter-city routes buying a return ticket can sometimes save money and ISIC card holders are entitled to a discount of 10% on fares costing more than 10 NIS.

Sherut

Sheruts, or service taxis, are usually stretch-Mercedes, seating up to seven passengers, or the little bug-like Volkswagen vans, which operate on a fixed route for a fixed price just like a bus. If you are uncertain about the fare, just ask your fellow passengers. Regular rates are normally about 20% more than the bus, but are sometimes on a par.

Most sheruts travel between towns and cities from recognised taxi ranks, departing when they're full. With a sherut you can get out anywhere along the way but you pay the same fare regardless. After dropping off a passenger the sherut then picks up replacement passengers wherever possible.

In the West Bank, where the Egged service is limited to Jewish settlements, the service taxis (in Arabic drop the 'taxi' bit and just say 'servees') are a better, faster alternative to the local Arab buses.

Sheruts also run on Shabbat when the religiously compliant Egged is off the road.

Train

The small passenger network of the Israel State Railways (IRS) is slightly cheaper than the buses but this is offset by its extremely limited scope and the generally inconvenient location of most railway stations, away from city and town centres. The train network, however, does pass through some delightfully scenic countryside, particularly the Tel Aviv to Jerusalem route.

ISRAELI MINISTRY OF TOURISM

You don't have to love olives to visit Israel, but it helps

ISIC holders get a 20% discount on all rail fares.

The main line is Haifa-Tel Aviv Central (North), used primarily by commuters. Some trains continue to Nahariya, via Akko, and there is a daily train running in each direction between Haifa and Jerusalem. Despite problems with outdated equipment, the level of service and comfort is generally acceptable if a little slow.

Car

Good roads, light traffic, beautiful scenery and short distances make Israel a great place to hire a car. Also, in places like the Golan and the Negev, the buses serve only a limited area and having your own vehicle can be a real boon. Even if you're on a tight budget, a few people sharing a car can be an economically viable way to see specific areas, if not the whole country.

ISRAELI MINISTRY OF TOURISM

Israel has a delicious selection of breads and filled pastries, both of Jewish and Arabic origin

In Israel you drive on the right-hand side of the road. Seat belts should be worn at all times by front-seat occupants. The speed limit is 50 km/h (31 mph) in built-up areas and 90 km/h (56 mph) elsewhere unless stated, but this is typically ignored – Israelis seem to exhibit near suicidal tendencies once behind the wheel, and more have been killed in road accidents than have died in all the wars with their Arab neighbours. Don't let this put you off but do be extra cautious.

Driving in the West Bank

Although the air is considerably less stone-filled than it was in the days of the intifada it is still not entirely advisable to drive a car with *yellow* Israeli licence plates in the West Bank (Arab licence plates are *blue*). Check your itinerary with the car hire company.

Bicycle

Cycling is a cheap, convenient, healthy, environmentally sound and above all fun way of getting around Israel. The same reasons, given above, that make the country great for driving also make it appealing for cycling; namely good roads with light traffic, some beautiful scenery and relatively short distances between the major towns and sights. Most major roads also have a hard shoulder, so cyclists can stay well clear of the traffic.

For flagging cyclists, interurban buses can usually accommodate bikes in their underslung luggage bays without any disassembly required; you'll probably be charged an additional 50% of the fare.

The main drawback to cycling in Israel is, of course, the heat. Always set off as early as possible, carry plenty of water (preferably chilled and in an insulator pack) and aim to finish for the day around early afternoon.

Choose your route carefully; while the coastal plain is flat enough, Upper Galilee, the Golan area and the Dead Sea Region have innumerable steep hills to be negotiated.

You will have to bring your own bike out with you because although a few places in Eilat, Jericho and Tiberias hire by the day their machines are unsuitable for long-distance riding.

Bicycles can travel by air. You *can* take them to pieces and put them in a bike bag or box, but it's much easier simply to wheel your bike to the check-in desk, where it should be treated as a piece of baggage. You may have to remove the pedals and turn the handlebars sideways so that it takes up less space in the aircraft's hold; check all this with the airline well in advance, preferably before you pay for your ticket.

Before you leave home, go over your bike with a fine-toothed comb and fill your repair kit with every imaginable spare, because the odds are 10-to-one you won't be able to buy that crucial gizmo you need to get you back on the road.

Comment Circuler en Israël et les Territoires Palestiniens

Bus

Israël est un pays relativement petit, qui bénéficie d'un excellent réseau routier, de sorte que le bus constitue le meilleur mode de transport.

Le réseau des bus israéliens est dominé par la tentaculaire compagnie Egged. Elle gère environ 4 000 véhicules sur plus de 3 000 itinéraires réguliers, ainsi que de nombreuses excursions spéciales. Les bus circulent fréquemment, sont rapides et bien entretenus. Il est conseillé de réserver pour vous rendre au bord de la mer Morte et dans le Négev, itinéraires sur lesquels Egged assure également le transport militaire, convoyant des soldats depuis ou vers leurs casernes.

La plupart des bus circulent tous les jours de 5h30 à 22h30 environ, mais méfiez-vous lors du Shabbat : le vendredi et la veille des fêtes juives, tous les bus, urbains et interurbains, roulent seulement jusqu'à 15h ou 16h, pour ne repartir que le samedi à la tombée de la nuit.

Le prix des bus israéliens a nettement augmenté mais reste intéressant. Le trajet le plus long qu'effectuent la plupart des voyageurs relie Eilat à Jérusalem (4 heures), ou Tel Aviv (5 heures), pour respectivement 42 et 46 NIS, soit environ vingt centimes français au kilomètre. Pour les voyages interurbains, il est parfois économique d'acheter directement un billet aller-retour, et une réduction de 10% est consentie aux détenteurs de la carte ISIC sur les trajets coûtant plus de 10 NIS.

Sherut

Le sherut, ou taxi collectif, est généralement une Mercedes limousine, qui peut accueillir jusqu'à sept passagers, ou un combi Volkswagen. Il circule sur un itinéraire déterminé pour un prix précis, de la même manière que les bus. Si vous avez un doute à propos du tarif, interrogez simplement les autres passagers. Les tarifs réguliers sont habituellement supérieurs de 20% environ à ceux des bus, mais dans certains cas, ils sont équivalents.

La plupart des sheruts sont postés dans les villes à des stations bien indiquées et partent lorsqu'ils sont pleins. Vous pourrez descendre n'importe où en route, mais le prix du billet restera le même. Après avoir déposé un passager, le conducteur du sherut attend dans la mesure du possible de pouvoir le remplacer.

En Cisjordanie, où les services d'Egged sont limités aux colonies juives, les taxis collectifs (simplement appelés "servees" en zone arabe) constituent une alternative meilleure et plus rapide aux bus arabes locaux.

Le sherut circule également durant le Shabbat, quand les bus Egged, conformément à la tradition religieuse, sont absents des routes.

Train

Le petit réseau ferroviaire passager des Israel State Railways (IRS) est légèrement moins coûteux que les bus, mais ses itinéraires sont très limités et la plupart des gares sont malencontreusement éloignées des centres-villes. Les trains traversent néanmoins quelques paysages merveilleux, notamment entre Tel Aviv et Jérusalem. Les détenteurs de la carte ISIC bénéficient de 20% de réduction sur tous les billets de train.

La ligne principale, entre Haifa et Tel Aviv Central (nord), est essentiellement utilisée par les banlieusards qui vont travailler. Certains trains poursuivent vers Nahariya *via* Akko (Saint-Jean d'Acre), et un train circule quotidiennement dans chaque sens entre Haifa et Jérusalem. Malgré des inconvénients dus à un matériel désuet, le service et le confort sont généralement d'un niveau acceptable, en dépit de la relative lenteur des trains.

Voiture

Les routes sont bonnes, la circulation n'est pas trop dense, les paysages sont superbes et les distances sont courtes, de sorte qu'Israël est un pays idéal pour louer une voiture. En outre, dans des sites comme le Golan et le Négev, les bus ne des-

ANDREW HUMPHREYS

A float in the Dead Sea is a must for any visitor to Israel and the Palestinian Territories

servent qu'une région limitée et un véhicule individuel peut s'avérer nettement plus intéressant. Même si votre budget est limité, il peut être plus économique de louer une voiture si plusieurs personnes la partagent pour visiter des régions spécifiques, voire l'ensemble du pays.

En Israël, on conduit à droite. Le port de la ceinture de sécurité est obligatoire partout pour les passagers des sièges avant. La vitesse est limitée à 50 km/h en agglomération et à 90 km/h ailleurs sauf indication contraire, mais rares sont ceux qui tiennent compte de ces limitations. Faites preuve de beaucoup de prudence.

Conduire en Cisjordanie

Même si les jets de pierres sont aujord'hui nettement moins fréquents qu'à l'époque de l'Intifada, il n'est toujours pas très recommandé de conduire une voiture portant des plaques d'immatriculation *jaunes* israéliennes en Cisjordanie (les plaques arabes sont *bleues*). Vérifiez votre itinéraire auprès de l'agence de location.

ANDREW HUMPHREYS

Church in Tabgha, on the shores of the Sea of Galilee

Bicyclette

Le vélo est un moyen de transport bon marché, pratique, sain, non polluant et surtout amusant ; les routes sont bonnes et peu encombrées, les paysages sont parfois superbes et les distances sont relativement courtes entre les villes et les sites principaux. La plupart des routes importantes sont également bordées de bas-côtés goudronnés, ce qui permet aux cyclistes de rester à l'abri de la circulation.

Il est facile de transporter les bicyclettes, qui tiennent généralement dans les soutes à bagages des bus interurbains sans qu'il soit nécessaire de les démonter ; dans ce cas, le prix du billet est habituellement majoré de 50%.

Le principal inconvénient à la pratique du cyclisme en Israël est bien sûr la chaleur. Partez toujours le plus tôt possible, emportez des réserves d'eau, et essayez de vous arrêter en début d'après-midi.

Choisissez soigneusement votre itinéraire ; si la plaine côtière est assez plate, la Haute Galilée, la région du Golan et celle de la mer Morte sont très vallonnées.

Vous devrez vous rendre en Israël avec votre propre bicyclette. En effet, même si quelques établissements à Eilat, Jéricho et Tibériade louent des vélos à la journée, ils ne conviennent pas aux longs trajets.

On peut transporter les bicyclettes par avion. Il est possible de les démonter et de les ranger dans un carton spéciale-ment conçu, mais il est bien plus facile de rouler simplement votre vélo jusqu'au comptoir d'enregistrement, où il sera considéré comme un bagage ordinaire. Vous devrez peut-être retirer le pédalier et tourner le guidon de côté pour qu'il tienne moins de place dans la soute de l'appareil ; renseignez-vous auprès de la compagnie aérienne avant votre départ, de préférence avant d'avoir payé votre billet.

Avant de partir, examinez très soigneusement votre bicyclette et préparez une trousse de secours aussi bien garnie que possible, car vous avez très peu de chances de trouver sur place cette petite pièce indispensable dont vous aurez besoin pour reprendre la route.

Reisen in Israel und den palästinensischen Gebieten

Bus

Aufgrund der relativ geringen Größe des Landes und der ausgezeichneten Busverbindungen sind Busreisen in Israel *die* Reiseart schlechthin.

Egged, nach Greyhound das zweitgrößte Busunternehmen der Welt, dominiert das israelische Bussystem. Das Unternehmen besitzt ungefähr 4.000 Busse, verkehrt auf über 3.000 regelmäßigen Routen und bietet zahlreiche Sonderreisen an. Die Busse fahren in regelmäßigen Abständen, sind flott und gut instand gehalten. Auf den Routen zum Toten Meer und die Negev Wüste ist es trotzdem ratsam seinen Sitzplatz im voraus zu reservieren, da Egged auf diesen Strecken auch als Militärtransporter agiert und Soldaten von und zu ihrer Basis schafft.

Die meisten Busse verkehren täglich zwischen ca. 5.30 Uhr und ca. 22.30 Uhr. Achten Sie jedoch auf Sabbat – an Freitagen und an den Vorabenden von jüdischen Feiertagen wird der Verkehr von allen städtischen und allen Intercity-Bussen zwischen 15.00 Uhr und 16.00 Uhr eingestellt. An Samstagen wird der Verkehr erst wieder nach Sonnenuntergang aufgenommen.

Busfahrten sind in Israel nicht mehr so spottbillig wie sie es einmal waren (was ist schon?), aber sie sind immer noch preiswert. Die längste Reise, die der Durchschnittsbesucher antritt, ist die Strecke zwischen Elat und Jerusalem (vier Stunden) oder Tel Aviv (fünf Stunden), die 42 bzw. 46 NIS kostet. Das entspricht ungefähr vier US Cents pro km. Der Kauf einer Rückfahrkarte kann auf Intercity-Strecken manchmal Geld sparen; Inhaber von ISIC-Ausweisen haben Anspruch auf eine 10%ige Ermäßigung bei Fahrpreisen über 10 NIS.

Sherut

Sheruts, oder Miettaxen, sind üblicherweise verlängerte Mercedes-Limousinen mit Sitzplätzen für bis zu sieben Passagieren oder kleine, `Käfer`-ähnliche VW-Lieferwagen. Sie fahren auf einer bestimmten Strecke, zu einem bestimmten Preis. Genau wie Busse. Sollten Sie sich über den Fahrpreis nicht ganz sicher sein, dann fragen Sie einfach die anderen Passagiere. Der reguläre Fahrpreis liegt normalerweise 20% höher als bei Busfahrten, doch das muß nicht immer der Fall sein.

Die meisten Sheruts pendeln zwischen Städten und Dörfern und fahren von markierten Taxistandplätzen ab wenn sie voll sind. Wenn Sie mit einem Sherut reisen, können Sie jederzeit unterwegs aussteigen. Sie zahlen jedoch trotzdem den gleichen Fahrpreis. Wenn Passagiere abgesetzt werden, wird der Sherut, wo immer möglich, Ersatzpassagiere aufnehmen.

Im Westjordanland, wo der Egged-Dienst auf jüdische Siedlungen beschränkt ist, sind die Miettaxen (auf Arabisch nennen Sie sie einfach 'Serviiies') eine billigere und schnellere Alternative zu den örtlichen arabischen Bussen.

Sheruts verkehren auch am Sabbat, wenn Egged, gemäß religiösen Gepflogenheiten, seinen Dienst eingestellt hat.

Zug

Das kleine Passagiernetz der staatlichen israelischen Bahn (IRS) kommt etwas billiger als Busse. Das extrem kleine Bahnnetz und die im allgemeinen ungünstige Lage der Bahnhöfe, weit weg von Stadt- und Dorfzentren, sind jedoch ein großer Nachteil. Die Züge fahren aber teilweise durch wunderschöne Landschaften, vor allem auf der Strecke von Tel Aviv nach Jerusalem. Inhaber von ISIC-Ausweisen bekommen eine 20%ige Ermäßigung auf alle Bahnpreise.

Die Hauptroute ist von Haifa nach Tel Aviv Zentrum (Nord). Diese Route wird in erster Linie von Pendlern in Anspruch genommen. Manche Züge fahren, über Akko, weiter nach Nahariya und es gibt auch einen Zug, der einmal täglich zwischen Haifa und Jerusalem in beide Richtungen fährt. Trotz mancher Probleme mit der altmodischen Ausstattung, sind Komfort und Service, wenn auch ein bißchen langsam, im allgemeinen akzeptabel.

Auto

Gute Straßen, wenig Verkehr, schöne Landschaften und kleine Entfernungen machen aus Israel einen idealen Platz zum Auto mieten. Dazu kommt noch, daß in Plätzen wie dem Golan und der Negev Wüste Busse nur sehr beschränkt verkehren. Das eigene Auto kann da zum wahren Segen werden. Wenn Sie gemeinsam mit mehreren Personen ein Auto mieten, kann das auch für Leute mit nur sehr limitierten Finanzen, ein billige Art sein, bestimmte Gegenden, ja selbst das ganze Land, zu erkunden.

In Israel fährt man auf der rechten Straßenseite. Passagiere auf den Vordersitzen sollten immer ihre Sicherheitsgurte anlegen. Das Tempolimit beträgt 50 km/h (31 mph) in verbauten Gebieten und, falls nicht anders angegeben, 90 km/h (56 mph) auf allen anderen Straßen. Doch Tempolimits werden grundsätzlich nicht beachtet - Israelis scheinen eine fast selbstmörderische Tendenz zu entwickeln sobald Sie sich hinter das Steuer setzen. Es starben bisher mehr Leute in Autounfällen als in allen Kriegen mit den arabischen Nachbarn zusammen. Lassen Sie sich davon nicht abschrecken, aber seien Sie doppelt vorsichtig.

Autofahren im Westjordanland

Obwohl die Luft dort erheblich weniger steinegefüllt ist als sie es in den Tagen der Intifada war, ist es immer noch nicht ratsam, ein Auto mit *gelber* israelischer Nummerntafel im Westjordanland zu fahren (arabische Nummerntafeln sind *blau*). Überprüfen Sie Ihre Reiseroute mit der Autovermietung im voraus.

Fahrrad

Radfahren ist eine billige, praktische, gesunde, umweltfreundliche und vor allem unterhaltsame Art in Israel zu reisen. Die obengenannten Gründe, die das Land großartig für's Autofahren machen, machen es auch reizvoll zum Fahrrad fahren; d.h., gute Straßen mit wenig Verkehr, schöne Landschaften und relativ geringe Entfernungen zwischen den wichtigsten Städten und Sehenswürdigkeiten. Die meisten Hauptstraßen haben auch eine Standspur, die es Radfahrern leicht macht, vom Verkehr Abstand zu halten.

Die erschöpften Radfahrer können ihre Fahrräder mit in die Intercity-Busse nehmen, welche die Räder, ohne sie auseinandernehmen zu müssen, in ihrem hängenden Gepäckraum unterbringen können; höchstwahrscheinlich wird man Ihnen einen 50%igen Aufschlag auf den Fahrpreis verrechnen.

Der größte Nachteil beim Fahrrad fahren in Israel ist natürlich die Hitze. Sie sollten immer so früh wie möglich los, sollten immer ausreichend Wasser mitführen (am besten gekühlt und in einer Kühltasche) und sollten es sich so einteilen, daß Sie irgendwann am frühen Nachmittag mit dem Radfahren aufhören können.

Wählen Sie Ihre Route sorgfältig; die Küstenebenen sind zwar flach, aber in Obergaliläa, auf den Golanhöhen und in der Gegend um das Tote Meer können Sie damit rechnen, unzählige Steigungen überwinden zu müssen.

Sie werden Ihr eigenes Fahrrad mitbringen müssen, denn obwohl einige Plätze in Elat, Jericho und Tiberias Fahrräder für einen Tag verleihen, sind diese für längere Touren völlig unbrauchbar.

Fahrräder können mit dem Flugzeug reisen. Sie *können* sie auseinandernehmen und in einer Fahrradtasche oder -box verstauen. Es ist jedoch viel einfacher, das Rad einfach zum Check-In-Schalter zu rollen, wo es als ganz normales Gepäck-stück behandelt werden sollte. Es kann nur sein, daß Sie die Pedale entfernen und die Handgriffe seitlich hochklappen müssen, sodaß es weniger Platz im Laderaum des Flugzeugs einnimmt; überprüfen Sie jedoch all das mit Ihrer Fluglinie im voraus - am besten bevor Sie das Ticket bezahlen.

Zuhause vor der Abfahrt, sollten Sie Ihr Fahrrad auf Herz und Nieren prüfen und Ihr Pannenset mit allen erdenklichen Ersatzteilen auffüllen. Denn die Chancen stehen 10 zu 1, daß Sie das notwendige, alles entscheidende Ding, daß Sie wieder fahrtüchtig macht, nirgendwo kaufen.

The Judean Desert

ANDREW HUMPHREYS

Cómo Movilizarse dentro de Israel y los Territorios Palestinos

En Autobús

Israel es un país relativamente pequeño. Esto, combinado con su excelente red de carreteras, hace que el viajar en autobús sea *la* mejor manera de movilizarse.

En Israel, el transporte por autobús está dominado por la compañía Egged, la segunda en importancia en el mundo después de la Greyhound. La compañía opera unos 4000 autobuses a lo largo de más de 3000 rutas programadas, además de muchos viajes especiales. Los autobuses son frecuentes, rápidos y están bien cuidados, pero les recomendamos que pidan reservas con anticipación para las rutas del Mar Muerto y Negev en las que Egged juega el doble papel de transportador militar llevando soldados que van y vienen de sus bases.

La mayoría de los servicios operan diariamente desde las 5.30 am hasta aproximadamente las 10.30 pm pero tenga cuidado con la Shabbat - los viernes y las vigilias de las fiestas judías todos los autobuses, urbanos e interurbanos, operan sólo hasta las 3 ó las 4 pm y los sábados no empiezan a funcionar hasta que se pone el sol.

El viajar en autobús en Israel ya no es la ganga que era antes (¿queda alguna?) pero continúa siendo barato. El recorrido más largo que la mayoría de los visitantes hacen es desde Eliat a Jerusalén (cuatro horas) o a Tel Aviv (cinco horas) que cuesta 42 y 46 NIS respectivamente, o unos 4 centavos americanos por km. En las rutas interurbanas el comprar un billete de ida y vuelta a veces puede ahorrarle dinero y los poseedores de la tarjeta ISIC tienen derecho a un descuento del 10% en los pasajes que cuesten más de 10 NIS.

En Sherut

Sheruts, o el servicio de taxis, generalmente se ofrece en mercedes alargados que pueden llevar hasta siete pasajeros, o bien en pequeñas furgonetas Volkswagen que operan en rutas fijas por precios prefijados al igual que los autobuses. Si usted no está seguro del precio del pasaje, pregunte a los otros viajeros. Por lo general, las tarifas son un 20% más caras que las del autobús aunque algunas veces son iguales.

La mayoría de los sheruts viajan entre los pueblos y las ciudades partiendo de lugares reconocibles como estaciones de taxis, y salen cuando están llenos. En un sherut, usted se puede apear en cualquier lugar a lo largo de la ruta, pero tiene que pagar el pasaje completo. Cuando se apea un viajero, el sherut toma otro si es posible.

En la Ribera Occidental donde los servicios de Egged son sólo para las colonias judías, los servicios de taxis (en árabe no hace falta decir 'taxi' diga solamente 'servis') son una alternativa mejor y más rápida a los autobuses árabes locales.

Los sheruts funcionan los días festivos, mientras que la compañía Egged cumple con sus principios religiosos y no opera esos días.

En Tren

Los precios en la pequeña red de ferrocarriles de Israel (IRS) son un poco más baratos que los autobuses, pero esto queda contrarrestado por el infrecuente servico y la ubicación en lugares inconvenientes de la mayoría de las estaciones, que quedan lejos de los centros de las ciudades y pueblos. Sin embargo, los trenes pasan por

ANDREW HUMPHREYS

Jews believe that prayers inserted into the Western Wall in Jerusalem have a better than average chance of being answered

algunos bellos parajes campestres, en particular la ruta de Tel Aviv a Jerusalén. Los poseedores de la tarjeta ISIC reciben un 20% de descuento en todos los pasajes de tren.

La ruta principal es Haifa-Tel Aviv Central (Norte), usada principalmente por los que viajan cada día. Algunos trenes continúan hasta Nahariya, vía Akko, y hay un tren diario que viaja en ambas direncciones entre Haifa y Jerusalén. A pesar de los problemas ocasionados por el equipo anticuado, el nivel de servicio y comodidad es por lo general aceptable, aunque un poco lento.

En Coche

Las buenas carreteras, el poco tráfico, los bellos paisajes y las distancias cortas hacen que Israel sea un lugar ideal donde alquilar un coche. Además, en lugares como Golán y Negev, los autobuses sirven solamente una zona limitada, por lo que tener disponible un vehículo es una gran ventaja. Aunque usted viaje con un presupuesto limitado, alquilar un coche junto con otras pocas personas puede ser una manera económicamente factible de visitar algunas zonas e incluso el país entero.

En Israel se viaja por la derecha de la carretera, Los pasajeros de los asientos delanteros deben llevar siempre puestos los cinturones de seguridad. La velocidad máxima permitida es de 50 km/h (31 mph) en las zonas urbanizadas y de 90 km/h (56 mph) en las otras zonas, a no ser que se indique la velocidad máxima, pero todo esto generalmete se deja de lado – los israelitas parece que tienen instintos casi suicidas cuando están detrás del volante, y el país ha sufrido más muertes en las carreteras que en todas las guerras contra las naciones árabes vecinas. No se asuste por esto, pero vaya con mucho cuidado.

Al Manejar en la Ribera Occidental

Aunque el aire está menos cargado que en los días de la intifada, no es todavía aconscjable viajar en un coche con matrícula *amarilla* israelí en la Ribera Occidental (las matrículas árabes son azules). Compruebe su itinerario con la compañía donde alquile el coche.

En Bicicleta

El viajar en bicicleta es barato, conveniente, saludable, no perjudica el medio ambiente y, sobre todo, es una manera divertida de movilizarse por Israel. Las razones que dimos antes que contribuyen a que el país sea adecuado para viajar en coche, hacen que lo sea también para los viajes en bicicleta; buenas carreteras y poco tráfico, algunos bellos paisajes y distancias relativamente cortas entre las poblaciones más grandes y los lugares inte-resantes. Además, muchas carreteras tienen los bordes duros y, por lo tanto, los ciclistas pueden ir apartados del tráfico.

Para los ciclistas flojos, los autobuses interurbanos normalmente pueden llevar las bicicletas, sin necesidad de desarmarlas, en el lugar destinado para el equipaje; probablemente tendrá que pagar un 50% adicional al costo del pasaje.

En Israel, el mayor inconveniente para los ciclistas es, naturalmente, el calor. Empiece el viaje tan temprano como pueda, lleve consigo mucha agua (preferiblemente fría en un recipiente aislador) y trate de terminar la jornada a media tarde.

Elija cuidadosamente la ruta; la región costera es bastante llana, pero la alta Galilea, la zona del Golan y la región del Mar Muerto tienen muchísimas cuestas empinadas que hay que vencer.

Usted tendrá que llevar su propia bicicleta puesto que aunque en algunos lugares como Eliat, Jericó y Tiberias se alquilan bicicletas para el día, estas no son adecuadas para viajes largos.

Las bicicletas pueden llevarse en el avión. Hay que desarmarlas y ponerlas en una bolsa o caja para bicicletas, pero es mucho más fácil rodarla hasta el mostrador de chequeo donde debe ser tratada como una pieza de equipaje. Quizás tenga que desmontar los pedales y girar el manillar para que ocupe menos sitio en la bodega del avión; pregunte todo esto a la compañía de aviación con bastante anticipación, preferiblemente antes de pagar por el pasaje.

Antes de salir de casa, repase la bicicleta con una lupa y llene la cartera de repuestos con todos los recambios que pueda imaginar porque existen 10 probabilidades contra una de que usted no podrá comprar esa cosita esencial que necesita para poder continuar en la carretera.

ANDHEW HUMPHREYS

One of the many quaint alleyways of Old Jaffa

イスラエルとパレスチナ領の旅

バス

イスラエルは国土が比較的小さく、道路交通網が大変発達しているため、最も便利なのはバスを使っての旅行だ。

イスラエルのバス路線網はグレイ・ハウンドに次いで世界で2番目に大きいバス会社であるエッゲド(Egged)が独占している。数多くの特別ツアー以外にも、3000以上の路線を約4000台のバスが定期運行している。バスは便数が多くて速く、整備が行届いている。しかし、死海(Dead Sea)とネゲブ(Negev)路線に関しては予約をしておくことを勧める。エッゲドは軍の運輸機関として軍備や兵士を基地の内外へと輸送するため便を倍増するからだ。

ほとんどの便は毎日午前5:30から午後10:30頃まで運行するが、シャバット(Shabbat：金曜日)とユダヤ教の祭日は、市街便、都市間連絡便ともバスはすべて午後3時か4時で終了し、土曜日の日没まで運行は再開しない。

ISRAELI MINISTRY OF TOURISM

The ancient Roman capital of
Caesarea

以前ほど格安ではなくなったが、イスラエルのバスはまだ割安なほうだ。平均的な旅行者が移動する最長距離はエイラット－イェルサレム間(Eilat-Jerusalem：4時間)、またはエイラット－テル・アビブ(Tel Aviv：5時間)間で、それぞれ42NISと46NIS。これは1kmあたり約4USセントに相当する。都市間連絡便の場合、往復切符のほうが割安のこともある。また、ISICカード(国際学生証)があれば10NIS以上の料金は1割引になる。

シェルート(Sherut)

シェルート、またはサービス・タクシーは、通常、車体を伸ばした乗客7人乗りのメルセデス・ベンツ、あるいは小型バスのようなフォルクス・ワーゲンのバンだ。これは、ちょうどバスのように路線と運賃が決まっている。料金がいくらかわからないときは気軽に他の乗客に聞くといい。運賃は通常バスよりも20%ほど割高だが、たまに値段が同じこともある。

ほとんどのシェルートは町や都市を結び、満員になり次第決まった発着場から出発する。シェルートは路線上であればどこでも下車できるが、下車した位置に関わらず料金は一定だ。途中で乗客が降りると道筋上であればどこでも次の乗客を拾う。

エッゲドのバスがユダヤ人居住地域しか運行していないウェスト・バンク(West Bank)では、サービス・タクシー(アラビア語では「タクシー」の部分を省略して、「サービス」とだけ発音する)のほうが現地のアラビアのバスよりも設備がよく、速い。

シェルートは宗教的に忠実なエッゲドがしばしば休みになるシャバットの時でも運行している。

電車

乗客網の小さいイスラエル国営鉄道(Israel State Railways: IRS)はバスより多少安いが、規模がたいへん限られている上、駅が町や都市の中心から離れた不便な場所にあることが多いので、良い交通手段だとは一概にはいえない。しかし、いくつかの線、特にテル・アビブ、イェルサレム間は、素晴らしい風景の田舎を走っている。ISICカードがあれば、すべての料金が2割引になる。

主要な線はハイファ(Haifa)－テル・アビブ・セントラル(北)で、主に通勤線として使われている。このうちいくつかの便はアッコ(Akko)経由でナハリヤ(Nahariya)まで行く。ハイファ－イェルサレム間は毎日両方向からそれぞれ便が一本出ている。スピードが少々遅く設備は古いが、サービスと乗り心地はまあまあ満足できる。

自動車

整備され渋滞の少ない道路、美しい風景、短距離旅程のため、イスラエルはレンタカーを借りて旅行するにはとてもいいところだ。また、ゴラン(Golan)やネゲブのような場所ではバスの路線が限られているので、自分で運転し移動できるのはとても快適だ。きつい予算でも、短い距離なら何人かと共同で車を借りて旅行すれば経済的だ。

イスラエルは右側通行だ。前部座席は常にシートベルト

を着用すること。制限速度は町中で時速50キロ（時速31マイル）、郊外で特に表示がなければ90キロ（56マイル）だが、普通これらは無視される－イスラエル人はハンドルを握ったとたん自殺的行為をする傾向があるようだ。交通事故の死亡者数は近隣のアラブ諸国間との戦争死亡者数よりも多い。だからといってあきらめずに、十分に気を付けて運転すること。

ウエスト・バンクを運転するとき
以前のインティファーダ（intifada：1987年末のイスラエル占領地でのパレスチナ人による反イスラエル占領闘争）の頃のように石を投げられるような緊張した雰囲気はないが、ウエスト・バンクでは現在でも黄色いイスラエルのナンバープレートの車（アラブのナンバープレートは青）の運転はなるべく避けたほうが良い。レンタカー会社の説明書を確かめること。

自転車
イスラエルの自転車旅行は、安くて便利、そして健康的で環境にやさしく、このうえなく楽しい。自動車の欄で述べたように、整備された道路、美しい風景、比較的短距離にある都市や見所など、この国を自転車で旅行することは自動車と同様に素晴らしい。ほとんどの主要道路は路肩がしっかりしているから、車線から十分に離れて自転車に乗ることができる。

　途中でギブアップしたサイクリストのため、通常、都市間連絡バスは自転車を分解しなくても床下の荷物室に入れて運べる。ふつう、半人分の乗車料金が加算される。

　イスラエルをサイクリングするのに唯一の欠点はその暑さだ。できる限り早めに行動を開始し、水を十分に持ち（冷やして断熱効果のある入れ物に入れると良い）、午後の早いうちにその日の行程を終わらせるようにするといい。

　ルートは気をつけて選ぶこと。海岸の平地はなだらかだが、ガリリー高地（Upper Galilee）、ゴラン地域（Golan）、死海地域では無数の険しい坂に挑まなくてはならない。

　エイラット、イェリコー(Jericho)、ティベリアス(Tiberias)では日数単位で貸自転車が借りられるが長距離向きではないので、自分の自転車を持ち込まなくてはいけない。

　自転車の空輸は可能だ。分解して自転車用バッグか箱に入れて運送できるが、チェック・イン・カウンターに分解せずに押していけば、荷物の一つとして扱ってくれるので、この方がずっと楽だ。場所をとらないように、ペダルをはずしハンドルを横にしなくてはいけないこともある。できれば航空券の支払いをする前に、あらかじめ航空会社に確認すること。

　家を出発する前に自転車の整備を綿密にし、修理キットの中にあらゆる部品を十分に揃えること。自転車旅行を続けるために必要となる部品は十中八九入手できないので。

GADI FARFOUR

Part of the mosaic of Jerusalem life, a Greek Orthodox priest and Oriental Jewish policeman

Index

Mt Harduf 26 D1
Mt Hardun 26 C2
Mt Harif 29 G6
Mt Harivi 14 A2
Mt Haroz 32 C2
Mt Hazak 11 H4
Mt Hazaron 26 D1
Mt Hazera 26 C6
Mt Hazofim 22 D2
Mt Hemda 33 F3
Mt Hemet 29 H5
Mt Hermonit 11 G3
Mt Hermonit Reserve 11 G3
Mt Hermon Shoulder 11 G1
Mt Hillazon 10 C6
Mt Hillel 10 D5
Mt Hison 32 C1
Mt Hizkiyahu 34 D5
Mt Hogen 34 D2
Mt Holed 26 D1
Mt Hordos 22 D4
Mt Horsha 29 G5
Mt Horshan 13 G4
Mt Horshan Reserve 13 G4
Mt Ikesh 11 H5
Mt Itai 26 D1
Mt Kabir 18 D3
Mt Kahal 11 G2
Mt Kal'an 10 D4
Mt Kamom 10 C6
Mt Kana'im 26 D2
Mt Karkom 32 C2
Mt Karmel 13 G2
Mt Katum 30 C5
Mt Kena'an 11 E5
Mt Kidod 26 D3
Mt Kipa 33 F2
Mt Kirton 30 B6
Mt Kishor 10 C5
Mt Kor 11 E6
Mt Kramim 11 G2
Mt Ksulot 14 B3
Mt Kurtam 11 H4
Mt Lehavim 25 H1
Mt Leta'ot 26 C2
Mt Loz 29 G6
Mt Mador 30 C2
Mt Makhbir 30 D6
Mt Malkishua' 14 C6
Mt Malkiya 11 E4
Mt Marpek 30 C5
Mt Marzeva 30 D3
Mt Masa 30 D5
Mt Masor 31 E3
Mt Mehalel 13 G3
Mt Mehilot 26 B2
Mt Meiron 10 D5
Mt Meiron Reserve 10 D5
Mt Menahem 26 D2
Mt Menorim 14 D2
Mt Michael 32 C2
Mt Mihya 30 A2
Mt Mikhrot 35 F3
Mt Montar 23 E3
Mt Na'ama 26 D2
Mt Na'azuz 33 E6
Mt Namer 26 D2
Mt Namron 15 F2
Mt Nebo (J) 23 H2
Mt Nekarot 30 D5
Mt Nes 32 B2
Mt Netofa 14 C1
Mt Nezer 11 E3
Mt Nezer Reserve 11 E3
Mt Nimra 14 C2
Mt Nishpe 30 D6
Mt Noter 11 E2

Mt 'Oded 29 H6
Mt Odem 11 G3
Mt Ora 35 E4
Mt Orahot 30 D3
Mt Oren 13 G2
Mt Parot 33 E6
Mt Peqi'in 10 C5
Mt Peres 11 H5
Mt Pitam 30 B5
Mt Rahama 25 H6
Mt Ram 11 G2
Mt Ramat Ziporim 29 H2
Mt Ramon 29 H6
Mt Ravid 10 D6
Mt Raviv 29 G2
Mt Rehav'am 34 D6
Mt Rekhev 30 C2
Mt Resisim 29 G3
Mt Retamim 30 A2
Mt Rotem 26 B5
Mt Rut 29 G2
Mt Sagi 32 B2
Mt Saharonim 30 C5
Mt Sansan 22 B3
Mt Sansana 25 H1
Mt Sapon 29 G2
Mt Saraf 26 C5
Mt Sasa 10 D4
Mt Savyon 14 D1
Mt Seguv 34 D3
Mt Sha'alav 33 F5
Mt Shaharut 35 F1
Mt Shahrur 33 E6
Mt Shalhevet 26 D4
Mt Shamai 10 D5
Mt Shani (E) 34 D4
Mt Shehoret 35 E5
Mt Shekhanya 14 B1
Mt Shezif 11 G2
Mt Shezor 10 C6
Mt Shizafon 33 F6
Mt Shlomo 35 E6
Mt Shmuel 22 C2
Mt Shokef 13 G3
Mt Shomera 10 B4
Mt Sifsufa 10 D5
Mt Sukha 22 A3
Mt Tabor 14 C3
Mt Tayasim 22 B2
Mt Teref 30 C3
Mt Timna' 35 E3
Mt Tir'an 14 C2
Mt Uziyahu 35 E4
Mt Warda 11 G2
Mt Ya'alon 33 G5
Mt Yahav 30 D4
Mt Yahel 26 C3
Mt Yakim 10 D5
Mt Yavne'él 14 D3
Mt Yedidya 35 E5
Mt Ye'elim 26 D3
Mt Yehoshafat 35 E6
Mt Yesha' 11 E4
Mt Yishai 23 E6
Mt Yoash 34 D5
Mt Yonatan 27 E2
Mt Yosifon 11 G4
Mt Yosifon Reserve 11 G4
Mt Yotvata 35 F2
Mt Zadok 11 E5
Mt Zafira 26 D2
Mt Zafrir 10 C5
Mt Zakif 11 E2
Mt Zameret 14 B3
Mt Zaror 30 B1
Mt Zayad 26 B5
Mt Zefahut 35 E6
Mt Zemer 11 E4

Mt Zenifim 32 D5
Mt Zeva'im 26 D5
Mt Zevul 10 C5
Mt Zfiya 11 E2
Mt Zin 30 D2
Mt Zin Reserve 30 D2
Mt Zuri'az 33 E2
Mt Zurim 26 D5
Mu'awiya 13 H5
Mughaiyir 14 C6
Mughaiyir 18 D5
Mughazi 20 C6
Mukhaiyam Fari'a 18 D2
Mukhmas 22 D1
Muqawir (J) 23 G5
Muqeibila 14 B5
Mura'abat Cave 23 E4
Musheirifa 14 A4
Musmus 14 A4
Mu'ta (J) 27 H4
Muthallath Al Arida (J) 19 G4
Muthallath Al Misri (J) 19 G4

Na'an 21 H1
Nabi Musa 23 F2
Nabi Saleh 18 B5
Nablus (Shechem) 18 C3
Nadiv Valley 13 G5
Nafha Plateau 30 B3
Nafha Range 30 A3
Nahala 21 G3
Nahal Above Reserve 26 D3
Nahal Admon 26 D5
Nahal Akev 30 B4
Nahal Akrabim 31 E1
Nahalal 14 A3
Nahal Alexander 13 F6
Nahal Alexander 17 H2
Nahal Alot 29 G4
Nahal al-Umran (J) 35 F6
Nahal Amazyahu 31 G1
Nahal 'Amos 22 D5
Nahal 'Amram 35 F5-E5
Nahal 'Amud 10 D5
Nahal Anaka 30 B6
Nahal 'Aner 22 B5
Nahal 'Anim 26 A3
Nahal 'Anot 21 H2
Nahal 'Aqrab 29 G4
Nahal 'Arud 32 D1
Nahal 'Arugot 23 E6
Nahal 'Arugot Ha'lli Reserve 22 H6
Nahal 'Asaron 35 E2
Nahal Ashalim 26 D5
Nahal 'Ashosh 31 E6
Nahal Atedim 25 G5
Nahal Avenat 23 F3
Nahal Barak 33 F2
Nahal Barkan 13 G5
Nahal Baruka 32 C2
Nahal Basar 25 F6
Nahal Be'er Hayil 25 G6
Nahal Beersheba 25 H3
Nahal Beit HaEmek 10 B5
Nahal Beit HaEmek Reserve 10 B5
Nahal Ben Ya'ir 27 E2
Nahal Besor 20 D6, 24 D1
Nahal Bezek 14 D6
Nahal Bezek Reserve 14 C-D6
Nahal Bezet 10 C4
Nahal Bezet Reserve 10 B4
Nahal Bik'atayim 34 D2
Nahal Bosem 33 F4
Nahal Daliya Reserve 13 H4
Nahal Dan 11 F2
Nahal Darga 22 D4, 23 E4
Nahal Dimona 26 C4
Nahal Dishon 11 E4

Nahal Dishon Reserve 11 E4
Nahal Dolev Reserve 22 B3
Nahal Doran 22 A5
Nahal Ein Hogla 23 F2
Nahal 'Enan Reserve 11 E4
Nahal 'En Gev 15 F2
Nahal Ela 29 H4
Nahal El Al 15 F1
Nahal Elisha 23 F1
Nahal Eshel 32 C4
Nahal Etek 35 E3
Nahal Evlayim 14 A1
Nahal Faza'el 19 E5
Nahal Garof 35 E6
Nahal Ga'ton 10 A5
Nahal Geror 25 E1-G1
Nahal Geva'ot 22 B3
Nahal Gidron 31 E3
Nahal Gilabon 11 F4
Nahal Girzi 33 E6
Nahal Gishron 34 D6
Nahal Guvrin 21 G3
Nahal Ha'Arava 31 G2
Nahal HaBesor Reserve 24 D2
Nahal Hadav 30 C6
Nahal Hadera 13 G-H6, 14 C6
Nahal Hallamish 27 E4
Nahal Hannun 20 D5
Nahal Harod 14 B4-D5
Nahal HaRo'e 30 A1
Nahal Hatira 31 E1
Nahal Hava 30 B3
Nahal Havarim 30 A2
Nahal Haviva 18 B1
Nahal Hawwa 30 C3
Nahal Hazazon 22 D5, 23 E5
Nahal Hazor 11 F4
Nahal Hemar 27 E4
Nahal Hemarit 26 D5
Nahal Hemda 33 F3
Nahal Hemdat 19 F2
Nahal Hermon 11 F2
Nahal Hermon Reserve 11 F2
Nahal Hevron 25 H2
Nahal Hevyon 30 C1
Nahal Hillazon 10 C6
Nahal Hion 33 E6-F4
Nahal Hursha 29 F2
Nahal Idan 31 F2
Nahaliel 18 B5
Nahalin 22 C3
Nahal 'Irit 18 D1
Nahal Iyon 11 E2
Nahal Iyon Reserve 11 E2
Nahal Kanaf 11 G6
Nahal Karkom 32 D2
Nahal Kedem 23 E6
Nahal Kenan 30 A6
Nahal Ketura 33 F6
Nahal Kezev 33 F4
Nahal Kezi'a 30 A6
Nahal Kidron 22 D3
Nahal Koshesh 31 E2
Nahal Kziv 10 B4-D5
Nahal Kziv Reserve 10 B4
Nahal Lakhish 21 F2
Nahal Lavan 24 D6, 29 H2
Nahal Loz 29 G6
Nahal Ma'azar 32 C1-D2
Nahal Marzeva 30 C4
Nahal Mashak 31 E3
Nahal Mashkhiyot 19 F1
Nahal Masor 31 F3
Nahal Matmor 30 C1
Nahal Mattat Reserve 10 C4
Nahal Me'arot Reserve 13 G3
Nahal Meqna 21 H2
Nahal Meshushim 11 F5

Ha'Igrot Cave 23 E6
HaKarmel Cave 13 G3
HaKemah Cave 27 E5
Hareitun Cave 22 D4
Hazan Caves 21 H5
Kabara Cave 13 G4
Keshet Cave 10 B4
Matmon Cave 27 E1
Me'arat 'Alma 11 E4
Me'arat Netifim 11 G1
Me'arat Nezer 11 E3
Me'arat Oren 13 G2
Me'arot Dalya 19 E5
Mura'abat Cave 23 E4
Namer Cave 10 B4
Netifim Cave 10 B5
Ornit Cave 13 G2
Rakefet Cave 13 H3
Rosh HaNikra 10 A4
Sarakh Cave 10 B4
Sfonim Cave 13 G2
Shua Caves 22 A4
Somek Cave 13 H3
Sorek Cave 22 B2
Teomim Cave 22 B3
The Blue Cave 13 F3
Yonim Cave 10 B6

CHURCHES
Beit Jimal 22 A3
Church of the Beatitudes 11 E6
Deir Hajle 23 F2
Mar Saba 23 E3
Qarantal Monastery 23 F1
Qasr al Yahud 23 G1
St Georges Monastery 23 E1
Tabgha 11 E6

DUNES
Agur Dunes 24 C-D6
Ashdod Dunes 21 F2
Haluza Dunes 24 D5-F4
Shunera Dunes 25 E-F6
Yavne Dunes 17 F6

JUNCTIONS & INTERCHANGES
Almog Jct. 23 F2
'Atlit Interchange 13 G3
Caesarea Interchange 13 F5
Golani Jct. 14 C2
Ha'Arava Jct. 26 D6
HaSharon Jct. 17 H1
Latrun Interchange 22 A1
Mahanayim Jct. 11 E5
Megiddo Jct. 14 A4
Mordechai Jct. 21 E4
Olga Interchange 13 F6
Rosh Pina Jct. 11 E5
Shikmona Interchange 13 G2
Tel Arad Jct. 26 C3
Yehudiya Jct. 11 F6
Yesud HaMa'ala Jct. 11 E4
Zemah Jct. 15 E3
Zichron Ya'acov Interchange 13 F4

MOSQUES
Nabi Musa 23 F2
Sheikh Kamel 19 E3

MOUNTAINS
Anim Mts 26 A2
A-Ras 18 A1
Arif Cliffs 30 B6
Barak Plateau 33 F2
Barnea Plateau 29 G4
Dimona Mts 26 B5

Ef'e Mts 26 B5
Gerofit Plateau 33 F6
Geva'ot Loven 33 G3
Gilboa Mts 14 C5
Giv'at Agodal 30 C6
Giv'at At 21 H5
Giv'at Barnea' 29 G4
Giv'at Bazaq 11 G6
Giv'at Doron 14 D1
Giv'at Gad 21 H5
Giv'at Gimer 21 H5
Giv'at Golani 15 E3
Giv'at HaMore 14 C4
Giv'at Homa 22 D3
Giv'at Kesharim 29 F2
Giv'at Mar'et 26 B2
Giv'at Menuha 33 F4
Giv'at Moran 21 H6
Giv'at 'Oqzar 21 H5
Giv'at Pu'a 35 E5
Giv'at Ra'af 30 B5
Giv'at Raglim 29 F2
Giv'at Refed 26 A5
Giv'at Shaul 22 D2
Giv'at Shfifon 26 C5
Giv'at Zafit 26 C5
Giv'at Zehavon 30 B6
Giv'ot Ga'at 25 H1
Giv'ot Lahav 25 H2
Giv'ot Qadmay 26 C5
Hadav Plateau 30 B6
Hadud Cliffs (Zuqe Haddud) 33 F2
Hagar Hills 29 F2
Har Ayelet 11 E5
Har Zavoa' 25 H5
Hatira Mts 30 B1
Hever Plateau 23 E6
Ira Mts 26 B2
Iron Hills 13 H5
Jebel A Debebis 18 D4
Jebel al-Daba (J) 31 H1
Jebel al-Duhykei (J) 35 H3
Jebel al-Mureyqiba (J) 35 H1
Jebel as-Sabha (E) 29 F3
Jebel Hureish 18 C1
Jebel Jalis 22 C5
Jebel Karifa (J) 35 G6
Jebel Nazeb Mul'an (J) 35 G5
Jebel Rahawat 18 D4
Jebel Suweiqa (E) 34 C2
Jebel Tamun 19 E2
Jebel Um Nezila (J) 35 G6
Karbolet Hararim 30 C5
Kevuda Hills 29 H2
Kidod Range 26 D3
Kipat Eshet 33 G2
Loz Cliffs 32 B1
Masraq Anage 23 E4
Meiron Mts 10 D5
Menuha Ridge (Rekhes Menuha) 33 F3
Mitzpe Arnon 23 E6
Mitzpe Sayarim 34 D2
Mizpe Kedem 22 H6
Mizpe Shelagim 11 G1
Moav Mountains (J) 27 G1
Mount of Olives 22 D2
Mt Adami 14 D2
Mt Addir 10 C5
Mt Afor 30 C5
Mt Akavya 11 E6
Mt 'Akbara 11 E6
Mt Akhman 10 B4
Mt Akrab 29 H4
Mt Alexander 14 A5
Mt Alon 13 G2
Mt 'Amasa 26 B2
Mt Amir 35 E5

Mt Amram 35 E5
Mt Arbel 14 D1
Mt Ardon 30 C4
Mt Argaman 35 F2
Mt 'Arif 29 H6
Mt Arikha 30 A4
Mt Arkov 30 A2
Mt 'Arod 29 H5
Mt Avisaf 26 B2
Mt Avishai 22 H6
Mt Avital 11 G4
Mt Avivim 10 D4
Mt Avnon 26 A6
Mt 'Ayarim 29 G5
Mt Ayit 33 F6
Mt 'Azmon 14 B1
Mt Badad 30 D5
Mt Bar'on 11 G3
Mt Bar Yohai 10 D5
Mt Batur 32 B2
Mt Beder 26 D1
Mt Bental 11 G3
Mt Ben Ya'ir 27 E2
Mt Berekh 35 E3
Mt Bezek 14 C6
Mt Birya 11 E5
Mt B'nei Rasan 11 H4
Mt Boker 29 H1
Mt Bosmat 34 D3
Mt Darga 31 E5
Mt Dayya 26 B4
Mt Dela'at 32 C2
Mt Devora 14 C3
Mt Dimon 26 B5
Mt Dishon 11 E4
Mt Dov 11 G1
Mt Dovev 10 D4
Mt Eldad 30 A3
Mt Eliezer 11 E4
Mt Eli'ezer 14 A2
Mt Enmar 30 D3
Mt 'Eshet 33 G2
Mt 'Eval 18 D3
Mt Evyatar 11 E4
Mt 'Ezem 26 A5
Mt 'Ezoz 29 G4
Mt Gadir 18 D1
Mt Gadna' 35 E4
Mt Gavnonim 26 C2
Mt Gavriel 32 C2
Mt Gerizim 18 C3
Mt Gershom 11 E4
Mt Gevim 31 E5
Mt Gezem 30 C5
Mt Gilo 22 C3
Mt Giyora 22 B3
Mt Gizron 29 G5
Mt Godrim 10 C4
Mt Golehan 30 D1
Mt Gorani 26 D2
Mt HaGelili 10 B4
Mt HaHalak 30 D2
Mt Halamish 32 C3
Mt Haluqim 25 G6
Mt HaMe'ara 32 B1
Mt HaMeshar 33 F1
Mt Hamran 29 G4
Mt Harduf 26 D1
Mt Hardun 26 C2
Mt Harif 29 G6
Mt Harivi 14 A2
Mt Haroz 32 C2
Mt Hazak 11 H4
Mt Hazaron 26 D1
Mt Hazera 26 C6
Mt Hazofim 22 D2
Mt Hemda 33 F3
Mt Hemet 29 H5

Mt Hermonit 11 G3
Mt Hermon Shoulder 11 G1
Mt Hillazon 10 C6
Mt Hillel 10 D5
Mt Hison 32 C1
Mt Hizkiyahu 34 D5
Mt Hogen 34 D2
Mt Holed 26 D1
Mt Hordos 22 D4
Mt Horsha 29 G5
Mt Horshan 13 G4
Mt Ikesh 11 H5
Mt Itai 26 D1
Mt Kabir 18 D3
Mt Kahal 11 G2
Mt Kal'an 10 D4
Mt Kamom 10 C6
Mt Kana'im 26 D2
Mt Karkom 32 C2
Mt Karmel 13 G2
Mt Katum 30 C5
Mt Kena'an 11 E5
Mt Ketura 33 F6
Mt Kidod 26 D3
Mt Kipa 33 F2
Mt Kirton 30 B6
Mt Kishor 10 C5
Mt Kor 11 E6
Mt Kramim 11 G2
Mt Ksulot 14 B3
Mt Kurtam 11 H4
Mt Lehavim 25 H1
Mt Leta'ot 26 C2
Mt Loz 29 G6
Mt Mador 30 C2
Mt Makhbir 30 D6
Mt Malkishua' 14 C6
Mt Malkiya 11 E4
Mt Marpek 30 C5
Mt Marzeva 30 D3
Mt Masa 30 D5
Mt Masor 31 E3
Mt Mehalel 13 G3
Mt Mehilot 26 B2
Mt Meiron 10 D5
Mt Menahem 26 D2
Mt Menorim 14 D2
Mt Michael 32 C2
Mt Mihya 30 A2
Mt Mikhrot 35 F3
Mt Montar 23 E3
Mt Na'ama 26 D2
Mt Na'azuz 33 E6
Mt Namer 26 D2
Mt Namrom 15 F2
Mt Nebo (J) 23 H2
Mt Nekarot 30 D5
Mt Nes 32 B2
Mt Netofa 14 C1
Mt Nezer 11 E3
Mt Nimra 14 C2
Mt Nishpe 30 D6
Mt Noter 11 E2
Mt 'Oded 29 H6
Mt Odem 11 G3
Mt Ora 35 E4
Mt Orahot 30 D3
Mt Oren 13 G2
Mt Parot 33 E6
Mt Peqi'in 10 C5
Mt Peres 11 H5
Mt Pitam 30 B5
Mt Rahama 25 H6
Mt Ram 11 G2
Mt Ramat Ziporim 29 H2
Mt Ramon 29 H6
Mt Ravid 10 D6
Mt Raviv 29 G2

Nahal Ashalim 26 D5
Nahal 'Ashosh 31 E6
Nahal Atedim 25 G5
Nahal Avenat 23 F3
Nahal Barak 33 F2
Nahal Barkan 13 G5
Nahal Baruka 32 C2
Nahal Basar 25 F6
Nahal Be'er Hayil 25 G6
Nahal Beersheba 25 H3
Nahal Beit HaEmek 10 B5
Nahal Ben Ya'ir 27 E2
Nahal Besor 20 D6, 24 D1
Nahal Bezek 14 D6
Nahal Bezet 10 C4
Nahal Bik'atayim 34 D2
Nahal Bosem 33 F4
Nahal Dan 11 F2
Nahal Darga 22 D4, 23 E4
Nahal Dimona 26 C4
Nahal Dishon 11 E4
Nahal Ela 29 H4
Nahal El Al 15 F1
Nahal 'En Gev 15 F2
Nahal Eshel 32 C4
Nahal Etek 33 E3
Nahal Evlayim 14 A1
Nahal Faza'el 19 E5
Nahal Garof 35 E6
Nahal Ga'ton 10 A5
Nahal Geror 25 E1-G1
Nahal Gidron 31 E3
Nahal Gilabon 11 F4
Nahal Girzi 33 E6
Nahal Gishron 34 D6
Nahal Guvrin 21 G3
Nahal Ha'Arava 31 G2
Nahal Hadav 30 C6
Nahal Hadera 13 G-H6, 14 C6
Nahal Hallamish 27 E4
Nahal Hannun 20 D5
Nahal Harod 14 B4-D4
Nahal HaRo'e 30 A1
Nahal Hatira 31 E1
Nahal Hava 30 B3
Nahal Havarim 30 A2
Nahal Haviva 18 B1
Nahal Hawwa 30 C3
Nahal Hazazon 22 D5, 23 E5
Nahal Hazor 11 F4
Nahal Hemar 27 E4
Nahal Hemarit 26 D5
Nahal Hemda 33 F3
Nahal Hermon 11 F2
Nahal Hevron 25 H2
Nahal Hevyon 30 C1
Nahal Hillazon 10 C6
Nahal Hion 33 E6-F4
Nahal Hursha 29 F2
Nahal Idan 31 F2
Nahal Iyon 11 E2
Nahal Kanaf 11 G6
Nahal Karkom 32 D2
Nahal Kedem 23 E6
Nahal Kenan 30 A6
Nahal Ketura 33 F6
Nahal Kezev 33 F4
Nahal Kezi'a 30 A6
Nahal Kidron 22 D3
Nahal Koshesh 31 E2
Nahal Kziv 10 B4-D5
Nahal Lakhish 21 F2
Nahal Lavan 24 D6, 29 H2
Nahal Loz 29 G6
Nahal Ma'azar 32 C1-D2
Nahal Marzeva 30 C4
Nahal Mashak 31 E3
Nahal Masor 31 F3

Nahal Matmor 30 C1
Nahal Meqna 21 H2
Nahal Meshushim 11 F5
Nahal Miflasim 21 E6
Nahal Mikhmas 22 D1
Nahal Milha 19 E1
Nahal Mishmar 26 D1
Nahal Moran 10 D5
Nahal Nablat 17 H5
Nahal Na'im 25 G4
Nahal Nekarot 30 B5-D5
Nahal Nemiya 31 E4
Nahal Neriyya 10 C5
Nahal Netafim 34 D5-E5
Nahal Nizana 24 C6
Nahal Nizuz 35 E4
Nahal Nizzana 29 F2-H4
Nahal Nov 15 G2
Nahal Og 22 D2-F2
Nahal Ohalim 32 D5
Nahal 'Omer 30 D6, 31 E5-6
Nahal 'Ovadya 13 G2
Nahal Paran 32 D4
Nahal Paran 33 G2
Nahal Pattish 25 E1-F2
Nahal Pehami 32 C6
Nahal Peres 26 D5
Nahal Poleg 17 G2
Nahal Qishon 13 H2-3
Nahal Qumran 23 E3
Nahal Ramon 30 A5
Nahal Raviv 29 G1
Nahal Rehem 35 E4-F2
Nahal Revivim 25 F5-G6
Nahal Roqqad (S) 11 H6
Nahal Rut 29 G2
Nahal Sa'ed 24 C1
Nahal Sal'it 30 D3
Nahal Salqa 20 C6
Nahal Sapon 29 H2
Nahal Sefamnun 11 F6
Nahal Sekhakha 23 E3
Nahal Sekher 25 G4-H5
Nahal Semekh 15 F1
Nahal Sha'alav 33 F5
Nahal Shahak 31 F3
Nahal Shahmon 35 E6
Nahal Shani 34 D3
Nahal Sharsheret 25 F2
Nahal Shazar 32 C3-D3
Nahal Shehoret 33 E6
Nahal Shekhem 18 A1
Nahal Shikma 21 E4-F5
Nahal Shila 18 A5
Nahal Shizaf 31 E4
Nahal Shizafon 33 E5
Nahal Shlomo 35 E6
Nahal Sho'alim 25 H6
Nahal Shuah 11 F4
Nahal Sidra 29 G1
Nahal Si'on 11 F2
Nahal Snir (L) 11 F2
Nahal Sorek 17 F6, 21 H2, 22 B-C2
Nahal Tamar 27 E6
Nahal Tanninim 13 G5
Nahal Tavor 14 D3-4
Nahal Te'enim 18 A2
Nahal Terashim 32 D1
Nahal Teref 30 D2
Nahal Timna 21 H3
Nahal Tirza 19 E3
Nahal Tkoa 22 D4
Nahal Tzipori 14 A-B2
Nahal Yahel 33 G5
Nahal Yamin 26 B6
Nahal Yarmouk (J) 15 E4-F3
Nahal Yarmouk (S) 15 G2
Nahal Yarqon 17 G4, 18 A4

Nahal Yasif 10 A6
Nahal Yattir 26 A2
Nahal Yavne'el 14 D2
Nahal Yehudiya 11 F6
Nahal Yetter 30 A3
Nahal Yiftah'el 14 C2
Nahal Zafit 26 D6
Nahal Zalmon 10 D6, 14 D1
Nahal Zarhan 30 C2
Nahal Zavitan 11 G5
Nahal Zbed 10 D5
Nahal Zemer 26 B3
Nahal Zenifim 32 D5
Nahal Zenifim 33 E4
Nahal Zihor 33 E3
Nahal Zin 27 E6, 30 A3-D2
Nahal Zvira 31 E4
Nahr el Litani (L) 10 D1-E1
Waddi Al-Morer 23 E2
Wadi Aalla'ne (S) 15 H2
Wadi Abo Sidra 19 E2
Wadi Abu ez Zighan (J) 19 H3
Wadi Abu Ghraba (J) 23 G1
Wadi Abu Qatarun 20 D6
Wadi Aish 18 C5
Wadi al Arab (J) 15 F3
Wadi al-Fidan (J) 31 H4
Wadi al-Gafi (E) 32 A6
Wadi al-Hasa (E) 34 C2
Wadi A-Natuf 22 D1
Wadi Anmar (J) 19 G4
Wadi A Sha'ar 18 D4
Wadi A Shami (J) 18 C3
Wadi Bazat El Paras (J) 19 G5
Wadi Dahal (J) 31 H2
Wadi El 'Arov 22 C4
Wadi El Basem 18 C1
Wadi El Hakem 18 B5
Wadi el Hasa (J) 27 F6
Wadi el Karak (J) 27 G2
Wadi Heidan (J) 23 G6
Wadi Hudeira (J) 27 G4
Wadi Husban (J) 23 G2
Wadi Ibn Hammad (J) 27 G2
Wadi 'Isal (Wadi Suleiman) (J) 27 G3
Wadi Kufrinja (J) 19 G2
Wadi Mujib (J) 23 G6
Wadi Parosh (J) 19 F4
Wadi Qan'a 18 C3
Wadi Qelt 23 E1
Wadi Salman (Nahal Eiyllon) 22 B1
Wadi Shallala (J) 15 H3
Wadi Taiyiba (J) 15 F5
Wadi Udheimi (J) 23 H2
Wadi Yabis (Nahal Yavesh) (J) 15 E6
Wadi Zarqa (J) 23 G4
Wadi Ziqlab (J) 15 F5

RUINS
Awja al-Fawqa 18 D6
Azmon (E) 29 E4
Beit Trumpeldor 14 C4
Belvoir Castle 14 D4
Capernaum 11 E6
Deir Qal'a 18 A5
Ein Hamarmar 26 D5
Hammam Az Zarqa (J) 23 H3
Hammat Gader 15 F3
Hashem Um Drag 22 D6
Havat 'Avrona 35 E5
Hurvat Abu Saukh 22 B4
Hurvat Abu Tulul 25 H4
Hurvat Alem al-Hoda 18 C3
Hurvat al-Hama 19 F1
Hurvat Al-Humodya 22 C3
Hurvat Ali ad-Din 13 H3

Hurvat al-Mazar 19 E4
Hurvat 'Almit 22 D2
Hurvat 'Amodim 14 C1
Hurvat 'Amudya 21 F6
Hurvat 'Anim 26 B1
Hurvat Arbel 14 D1
Hurvat Aristubolya 22 C6
Hurvat 'At'ab 22 B3
Hurvat Batir 22 C3
Hurvat Bazir 10 C4
Hurvat Beer Resisim 29 G2
Hurvat Beersheba 10 D6
Hurvat Be'er Sherna 25 E2
Hurvat Beit El 18 C6
Hurvat Beit Horon Elyon 22 C1
Hurvat Benaya 21 H6
Hurvat Brekhot 22 C4
Hurvat Brekhot Shlomo 22 C3
Hurvat Dabla 13 G3
Hurvat Dardar 18 A2
Hurvat Dereg 13 H3
Hurvat Dragut 26 B2
Hurvat 'Ein Kovshim 10 A4
Hurvat Eshtemoa 26 B1
Hurvat Ga'ton 10 B5
Hurvat Giv'on 22 C1
Hurvat Gosh-Halave 10 D5
Hurvat Gvol 14 D4
Hurvat Halokm 30 B1
Hurvat Hanita 10 B4
Hurvat Hanut 22 B3
Hurvat Haraza 17 H2
Hurvat Hasif 25 E2
Hurvat Hermesh 13 H3
Hurvat Hurpa 21 H5
Hurvat Kafr Atia 18 D4
Hurvat Kahal 26 B2
Hurvat Karnei Hittim 14 D2
Hurvat Kefar 'Aziz 22 B6
Hurvat Kerem Abu Tabaq 23 E3
Hurvat Keroa' 21 H4
Hurvat Kfar Otnan 14 A4
Hurvat Kfar Se'ora 21 F5
Hurvat Kishor 21 H6
Hurvat Lezifar 26 B1
Hurvat Ma'ar 10 B4
Hurvat Manot 10 A5
Hurvat Ma'on 22 C6
Hurvat Ma'on 24 C2
Hurvat Masrafe 10 A4
Hurvat Matar 25 G3
Hurvat Mazar 14 C5
Hurvat Mazor 17 H5
Hurvat Merot 11 E5
Hurvat Migdal Afeq 17 H4
Hurvat Mimlah 14 D1
Hurvat Muhraqa 13 H3
Hurvat Na'aran 19 E6
Hurvat Nabi Roben 17 F6
Hurvat Nakik 21 H5
Hurvat Nappah 11 G4
Hurvat Nashe 18 A3
Hurvat Nekarot 30 D5
Hurvat Pi Mazzuva 10 A4
Hurvat Qasr Khalifa 22 C5
Hurvat Regem Zohar 26 D3
Hurvat Ritma 30 A1
Hurvat Safai 25 G3
Hurvat Saharonim 30 C5
Hurvat Sansan 22 B3
Hurvat Sasay 13 H2, 14 A2
Hurvat Se'adim 22 C3
Hurvat Sera 18 D5
Hurvat Serak 13 H3
Hurvat Shev'a 22 D4
Hurvat Siv 18 A1
Hurvat Sufa 25 F2
Hurvat Sukha 22 A3

Hurvat Suseya 22 B6
Hurvat Talimon 13 G4
Hurvat Tawila 13 H5
Hurvat Tel 18 C6
Hurvat Timna' 35 E3
Hurvat Tuqu' 22 C4
Hurvat 'Uza 26 C3
Hurvat Vradim 14 D1
Hurvat Yanun 18 D3
Hurvat Yatir 26 B1
Hurvat Yavne Yam 17 F6
Hurvat Yiftah'el 14 A2
Hurvat Zafir 31 E1
Hurvat Zafzafot 14 C3
Hurvat Zalmon 10 D6
Hurvat Zif 22 C6
Karmil 22 B6
Kerem Samra 23 E3
Keren Naftali 11 E4
Maqti'a 'Abud 18 A5
Masor Canyon 31 E3
Mazad Bokek 27 E3
Mazad Gozal 27 E3
Mazad Hatrurim 26 D3
Mazad Hazeva 31 F2
Mazad Mahmal 30 C3
Mazad Yeruham 25 H6
Mazad Yorke'am 26 B6
Mezodat Yesh'a 11 E4
Mezudat Har Raviv 29 G2
Mezudat Hemet 29 H4
Mitzpe Shivta 25 E6
Mivzar Latrun 22 A1
Montfort Castle 10 B4
Nevi'ot Heimar 27 E4
Pella (J) 15 E6
Q'ail'a 22 A4
Rogem Zafir 31 E1
Rugem Hillel 22 B5
Sodom 27 E5
Tel Adami 14 C2

Tel Agra 21 H5
Tel al-Fari'a 18 D2
Tel 'Ar'aur 26 A4
Tel Ashraf 17 G3
Tel Asraf 17 H1
Tel 'Azeqa 21 H3
Tel Batash 21 H2
Tel Beit Mirsham 21 H6
Tel Bet Shemesh 22 A3
Tel Dotan 14 B6
Tel 'Erani 21 G4
Tel 'Eton 21 H6
Tel Gama 24 D1
Tel Gat Hefer 14 B2
Tel Girit 13 F6
Tel Hai 11 E2
Tel Hannaton 14 B2
Tel Hazor 11 E5
Tel Hefer 17 H1
Tel 'Irit 21 E5
Tel Jatt 13 H6
Tel Kadesh 11 E4
Tel Kaner 17 G4
Tel Kison 10 A6
Tel Mahoz 17 F6
Tel Malot 21 H1
Tel Maresha 21 H4
Tel Mefalsim 21 E5
Tel Mifsah 21 F6
Tel Mikne 21 H2
Tel Milha 21 G6
Tel Mohelhol 23 F2
Tel Na'ama Reserve 11 F3
Tel Nizana 29 F2
Tel Peha 15 E5
Tel Regev 13 H2
Tel Rehov 14 D6
Tel Rekhesh 14 D3
Tel Shadod 14 B3
Tel Shaharit 15 E3
Tel Sharuhen 24 D2

Tel Shekef 21 F5
Tel Shihan 21 E6
Tel Shikmona 13 G1
Tel Shilo 18 D5
Tel Shosh 13 H4
Tel Ti'innik 14 A5
Tel Yarmut 22 A3
Tel Yisakhar 14 D4
Tel Yona 17 F5
Tel Zafit 21 G3
Tel Zor'a 22 A2
Tel Zoran 17 H2
Tel Zror 13 G6

VALLEYS & PLAINS
Ami'az Plain 27 E5
Arad Valley 26 C3
Ardon Valley 30 C4
Ayalon Valley 22 A1
Beit Kerem Valley 10 C6
Beit Netofa Valley 14 B1
Beit Zeida Valley 11 F6
Berakha Valley 22 B4
Bezek Valley 14 D6
Dotan Valley 14 B6
Ela Valley 22 A3
El Lisan (J) 27 F2
Harod Valley 14 D5
Hefer Valley 13 G6
Hion Plain 33 F4
Hula Valley 11 F3
Jericho Valley 23 F1
Jezreel Valley 14 A3
Kadesh Valley 11 E4
Kana'im Valley 26 D2
Ketura Valley 33 F6
Korha Valley 29 G1
Ksulot Valley 14 B-C3
Maharal Valley 13 G3
Mahmal Valley 30 C3
Moav Valley (J) 23 G2

Nadiv Valley 13 G5
Ovda Valley 33 F6
Paran Plain 32 C5
Rotem Plain 26 C5
Sakhnin Valley 10 C6
Sanur Valley 18 D1
Sara Valley 25 G3
Sayarim Valley 34 D3
Shilo Valley 18 D5
Sodom Valley 27 E6
Tamun Valley 19 E2
Timna Valley 35 E3
Wadi Araba (J) 31 F5
Yafruq Valley 33 G4
Yamin Plain 26 C6
Yavne'el Valley 14 D2
Zahiha Valley 33 E4
Zenifim Valley 32 D5
Zeva'im Valley 26 D5
Zin Valley 30 B2
Zohar Valley 27 E4
Zvulun Valley 10 A6

VIEWPOINTS
Mitzpe Amram 35 E5
Mitzpe Gilboa 14 C5
Mitzpe Ofir 15 F1
Mizpe Afik 15 F2
Mizpe HaOn 15 E2

WATERFALLS
Banias 11 F2
Devora 11 G4
Gamla 11 G6
Gilabon 11 F4
HaTanur Fall 11 E2
Mazukim Waterfall 26 C6
Meshoshim 11 F6
Resisim 11 G2
Sa'ar 11 G2
White Falls 15 F1

PLANET TALK

Lonely Planet's FREE quarterly newsletter

We love hearing from you and think you'd like to hear from us.

When...is the right time to see reindeer in Finland?
Where...can you hear the best palm-wine music in Ghana?
How...do you get from Asunción to Areguá by steam train?
What...is the best way to see India?

For the answer to these and many other questions read PLANET TALK.

Every issue is packed with up-to-date travel news and advice including:

* a letter from Lonely Planet co-founders Tony and Maureen Wheeler
* go behind the scenes on the road with a Lonely Planet author
* feature article on an important and topical travel issue
* a selection of recent letters from travellers
* details on forthcoming Lonely Planet promotions
* complete list of Lonely Planet products

To join our mailing list contact any Lonely Planet office.

Also available: Lonely Planet T-shirts. 100% heavyweight cotton.

LONELY PLANET ONLINE

Get the latest travel information before you leave or while you're on the road

Whether you've just begun planning your next trip, or you're chasing down specific info on currency regulations or visa requirements, check out the Lonely Planet World Wide Web site for up-to-the-minute travel information.

As well as travel profiles of your favourite destinations (including interactive maps and full-colour photos), you'll find current reports from our army of researchers and other travellers, updates on health and visas, travel advisories, and the ecological and political issues you need to be aware of as you travel.

There's an online travellers' forum (the Thorn Tree) where you can share your experiences of life on the road, meet travel companions and ask other travellers for their recommendations and advice. We also have plenty of links to other Web sites useful to independent travellers.

With tens of thousands of visitors a month, the Lonely Planet Web site is one of the most popular on the Internet and has won a number of awards including GNN's Best of the Net travel award.

http://www.lonelyplanet.com

LONELY PLANET GUIDES TO THE MIDDLE EAST

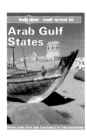

Arab Gulf States
This comprehensive, practical guide to travel in the Arab Gulf States covers travel in Bahrain, Kuwait, Oman, Qatar, Saudi Arabia and the United Arab Emirates. A concise history and language section is included for each country.

Iran
As well as practical travel details, the author provides background information that will fascinate adventurers and armchair travellers alike.

Israel & the Palestinian Territories
Journey back thousands of years exploring the sites that have inspired the world's major regions; float on the Dead Sea; go camel trekking in the Negev; volunteer for a unique kibbutz experience; and explore the holy city of Jerusalem and cosmopolitan Tel Aviv. This guide is packed with insight and practical information for all budgets.

Jordan & Syria
Two countries with a wealth of natural and historical attractions for the adventurous travellers...12th century Crusader castles, ruined cities and haunting desert landscapes.

Middle East on a shoestring
All the travel advice and essential information for travel in Afghanistan, Bahrain, Egypt, Iran, Iraq, Israel, Jordan, Kuwait, Lebanon, Oman, Qatar, Saudi Arabia, Syria, Turkey, United Arab Emirates and Yemen.

Trekking in Turkey
Explore beyond Turkey's coastline and you will be surprised to discover that Turkey has mountains to rival those found in Nepal.

Turkey
Experience Turkey with this highly-acclaimed, best selling guide. Packed with information for the traveller on any budget, it's your essential companion.

Turkish phrasebook
Practical words and phrases and a handy pronunciation guide, make this phrasebook essential for travellers visiting Turkey.

Yemen
Discover the timeless history and intrigue of the land of the *Arabian Nights* with the most comprehensive guide to Yemen.

Also available:

The Gates of Damascus by Lieve Joris (translated by Sam Garrett)
This best-selling book is a beautifully drawn portrait of day-to-day life in modern Syria. Through her intimate contact with local people, Lieve Joris draws us into the fascinating world that lies behind the gates of Damascus.

LONELY PLANET PRODUCTS

AFRICA
Africa on a shoestring • Arabic (Moroccan) phrasebook • Cape Town city guide • Central Africa • East Africa • Egypt • Egypt travel atlas • Ethiopian (Amharic) phrasebook • Kenya • Morocco • North Africa • South Africa, Lesotho & Swaziland • Swahili phrasebook • Trekking in East Africa• West Africa • Zimbabwe, Botswana & Namibia • Zimbabwe, Botswana & Namibia travel atlas

ANTARCTICA
Antarctica

AUSTRALIA & THE PACIFIC
Australia • Australian phrasebook • Bushwalking in Australia • Bushwalking in Papua New Guinea • Fiji • Fijian phrasebook • Islands of Australia's Great Barrier Reef • Melbourne city guide • Micronesia • New Caledonia • New South Wales & the ACT • New Zealand • Northern Territory • Outback Australia • Papua New Guinea • Papua New Guinea phrasebook • Queensland • Rarotonga & the Cook Islands • Samoa • Solomon Islands • South Australia • Sydney city guide • Tahiti & French Polynesia • Tasmania • Tonga • Tramping in New Zealand • Vanuatu • Victoria • Western Australia
Travel Literature: Islands in the Clouds • Sean & David's Long Drive

CENTRAL AMERICA & THE CARIBBEAN
Central America on a shoestring • Costa Rica • Eastern Caribbean • Guatemala, Belize & Yucatán: La Ruta Maya • Jamaica

EUROPE
Austria • Baltic States & Kaliningrad • Baltics States phrasebook • Britain • Central Europe on a shoestring • Central Europe phrasebook • Czech & Slovak Republics • Denmark • Dublin city guide • Eastern Europe on a shoestring • Eastern Europe phrasebook • Finland • France • Greece • Greek phrasebook • Hungary • Iceland, Greenland & the Faroe Islands • Ireland • Italy • Mediterranean Europe on a shoestring • Mediterranean Europe phrasebook • Paris city guide • Poland • Prague city guide • Russia, Ukraine & Belarus • Russian phrasebook • Scandinavian & Baltic Europe on a shoestring • Scandinavian Europe phrasebook • Slovenia • St Petersburg city guide • Switzerland • Trekking in Greece • Trekking in Spain • Ukrainian phrasebook • Vienna city guide • Walking in Switzerland • Western Europe on a shoestring • Western Europe phrasebook

INDIAN SUBCONTINENT
Bangladesh • Bengali phrasebook • Delhi city guide • Hindi/Urdu phrasebook • India • India & Bangladesh travel atlas • Indian Himalaya • Karakoram Highway • Nepal • Nepali phrasebook • Pakistan • Sri Lanka • Sri Lanka phrasebook • Trekking in the Indian Himalaya • Trekking in the Nepal Himalaya
Travel Literature: Shopping for Buddhas

ISLANDS OF THE INDIAN OCEAN
Madagascar & Comoros • Maldives & Islands of the East Indian Ocean • Mauritius, Réunion & Seychelles

MIDDLE EAST & CENTRAL ASIA
Arab Gulf States • Arabic (Egyptian) phrasebook • Central Asia • Iran • Israel & the Palestinian Territories • Israel & the Palestinian Territories travel atlas • Jordan & Syria • Jordan, Syria & Lebanon travel atlas • Middle East • Turkey • Turkish phrasebook • Trekking in Turkey • Yemen
Travel Literature: The Gates of Damascus

NORTH AMERICA
Alaska • Backpacking in Alaska • Baja California • California & Nevada • Canada • Hawaii • Honolulu city guide • Los Angeles city guide • Mexico • Miami city guide • New England • Pacific Northwest USA • Rocky Mountain States • San Francisco city guide • Southwest USA • USA phrasebook

NORTH-EAST ASIA
Beijing city guide • Cantonese phrasebook • China • Hong Kong city guide • Hong Kong, Macau & Canton • Japan • Japanese phrasebook • Japanese audio pack • Korea • Korean phrasebook • Mandarin phrasebook • Mongolia • Mongolian phrasebook • North-East Asia on a shoestring • Seoul city guide • Taiwan • Tibet • Tibet phrasebook • Tokyo city guide
Travel Literature: Lost Japan

SOUTH AMERICA
Argentina, Uruguay & Paraguay • Bolivia • Brazil • Brazilian phrasebook • Buenos Aires city guide • Chile & Easter Island • Chile travel atlas • Colombia • Ecuador & the Galápagos Islands • Latin American Spanish phrasebook • Peru • Quechua phrasebook • Rio de Janeiro city guide • South America on a shoestring • Trekking in the Patagonian Andes • Venezuela
Travel Literature: Full Circle: A South American Journey

SOUTH-EAST ASIA
Bali & Lombok • Bangkok city guide • Burmese phrasebook• Cambodia • Ho Chi Minh city guide • Indonesia • Indonesian phrasebook • Indonesian audio pack • Jakarta city guide • Java • Laos • Laos travel atlas • Lao phrasebook • Malaysia, Singapore & Brunei • Myanmar (Burma) • Philippines • Pilipino phrasebook • Singapore city guide • South-East Asia on a shoestring • Thailand • Thailand travel atlas • Thai phrasebook • Thai Hill Tribes phrasebook • Thai audio pack • Vietnam • Vietnamese phrasebook • Vietnam travel atlas

LONELY PLANET TRAVEL ATLASES

Conventional fold-out maps work just fine when you're planning your trip on the kitchen table, but have you ever tried to use one – or the half-dozen you sometimes need to cover a country – while you're actually on the road? Even if you have the origami skills necessary to unfold the sucker, you know that flimsy bit of paper is not going to last the distance.

"Lonely Planet travel atlases are designed to make it through your journey in one piece – the sturdy book format is based on the assumption that since all travellers want to make it home without punctures, tears or wrinkles, the maps they use should too."

The travel atlases contain detailed, colour maps that are checked on the road by our travel authors to ensure their accuracy. Place name spellings are consistent with our associated guidebooks, so you can use the atlas and the guidebook hand in hand as you travel and find what you are looking for. Unlike conventional maps, each atlas has a comprehensive index, as well as a detailed legend and helpful 'getting around' sections translated into five languages. Sorry, no free steak knives...

Features of this series include:

- full-colour maps, plus colour photos
- maps researched and checked by Lonely Planet authors
- place names correspond with Lonely Planet guidebooks, so there are no confusing spelling differences
- complete index of features and place names
- atlas legend and travelling information presented in five languages: English, French, German, Spanish and Japanese

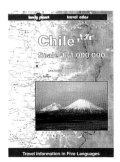

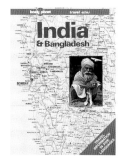

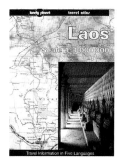

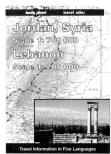

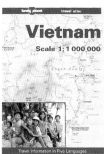

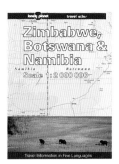

THE LONELY PLANET STORY

Lonely Planet published its first book in 1973 in response to the numerous 'How did you do it?' questions Maureen and Tony Wheeler were asked after driving, bussing, hitching, sailing and railing their way from England to Australia.

Written at a kitchen table and hand collated, trimmed and stapled, *Across Asia on the Cheap* became an instant local bestseller, inspiring thoughts of another book.

Eighteen months in South-East Asia resulted in their second guide, *South-East Asia on a shoestring*, which they put together in a backstreet Chinese hotel in Singapore in 1975. The 'yellow bible', as it quickly became known to backpackers around the world, soon became *the* guide to the region. It has sold well over half a million copies and is now in its 8th edition, still retaining its familiar yellow cover.

Today there are over 180 titles, including travel guides, walking guides, language kits & phrasebooks, travel atlases and travel literature. The company is one of the largest travel publishers in the world. Although Lonely Planet initially specialised in guides to Asia, we now cover most regions of the world, including the Pacific, North America, South America, Africa, the Middle East and Europe.

The emphasis continues to be on travel for independent travellers. Tony and Maureen still travel for several months of each year and play an active part in the writing, updating and quality control of Lonely Planet's guides.

They have been joined by over 70 authors and 170 staff at our offices in Melbourne (Australia), Oakland (USA), London (UK) and Paris (France). Travellers themselves also make a valuable contribution to the guides through the feedback we receive in thousands of letters each year.

The people at Lonely Planet strongly believe that travellers can make a positive contribution to the countries they visit, both through their appreciation of the countries' culture, wildlife and natural features, and through the money they spend. In addition, the company makes a direct contribution to the countries and regions it covers. Since 1986 a percentage of the income from each book has been donated to ventures such as famine relief in Africa; aid projects in India; agricultural projects in Central America; Greenpeace's efforts to halt French nuclear testing in the Pacific; and Amnesty International.

'I hope we send people out with the right attitude about travel. You realise when you travel that there are so many different perspectives about the world, so we hope these books will make people more interested in what they see.'

– Tony Wheeler

LONELY PLANET PUBLICATIONS

AUSTRALIA (HEAD OFFICE)
PO Box 617, Hawthorn 3122, Victoria
tel: (03) 9819 1877   fax: (03) 9819 6459
e-mail: talk2us@lonelyplanet.com.au

UK
10 Barley Mow Passage,
Chiswick, London W4 4PH
tel: (0181) 742 3161   fax: (0181) 742 2772
e-mail: 100413.3551@compuserve.com

USA
Embarcadero West,155 Filbert St, Suite 251,
Oakland, CA 94607
tel: (510) 893 8555   TOLL FREE: 800 275-8555
fax: (510) 893 8563
e-mail: info@lonelyplanet.com

FRANCE
71 bis rue du Cardinal Lemoine, 75005 Paris
tel: 1 44 32 06 20   fax: 1 46 34 72 55
e-mail: 100560.415@compuserve.com

World Wide Web: http://www.lonelyplanet.com/

ISRAEL & THE PALESTINIAN TERRITORIES TRAVEL ATLAS

Dear Traveller,

We would appreciate it if you would take the time to write your thoughts on this page and return it to a Lonely Planet office.
Only with your help can we continue to make sure this atlas is as accurate and travel-friendly as possible.

Where did you acquire this atlas?

Bookstore ☐   In which section of the store did you find it, i.e. maps or travel guidebooks? ....

Map shop ☐   Direct mail ☐   Other ....

How are you using this travel atlas?

On the road ☐   For home reference ☐   For business reference ☐

Other ....

When travelling with this atlas, did you find any inaccuracies?

....

....

....

How does the atlas fare on the road in terms of ease of use and durability?

Are you using the atlas in conjunction with an LP guidebook/s?   Yes ☐   No ☐

Which one/s?...

Have you bought any other LP products for your trip?...

Do you think the information on the travel atlas maps is presented clearly?   Yes ☐   No ☐

If English is not your main language, do you find the language sections useful?   Yes ☐   No ☐

Please list any features you think should be added to the travel atlas.

....

....

....

Would you consider purchasing another atlas in this series?   Yes ☐   No ☐

Please indicate your age group.

15-25 ☐   26-35 ☐   36-45 ☐   46-55 ☐   56-65 ☐   66+ ☐

Do you have any other general comments you'd like to make?

....

....

....

....

....

P.S. Thank you very much for this information. The best contributions will be rewarded with a free copy of a Lonely Planet book.
We give away lots of books, but, unfortunately, not every contributor receives one.